Maurice Francis Egan

Studies in literature

Some words about Chaucer, and other essays

Maurice Francis Egan

Studies in literature
Some words about Chaucer, and other essays

ISBN/EAN: 9783741179525

Manufactured in Europe, USA, Canada, Australia, Japa

Cover: Foto ©Andreas Hilbeck / pixelio.de

Manufactured and distributed by brebook publishing software
(www.brebook.com)

Maurice Francis Egan

Studies in literature

STUDIES IN LITERATURE.

SOME WORDS ABOUT CHAUCER
AND OTHER ESSAYS

BY

MAURICE FRANCIS EGAN, A. M., LL. D.

PROFESSOR OF ENGLISH LANGUAGE AND LITERATURE IN
THE CATHOLIC UNIVERSITY OF AMERICA.

B. HERDER
17 SOUTH BROADWAY, ST. LOUIS, MO.
AND
68 GREAT RUSSELL ST., LONDON, W.C.
1916

—BECKTOLD—
PRINTING AND BOOK MFG. CO.
ST. LOUIS, MO.

PROEM.

The essays comprised in this book might have been called "studies for lectures," — as such they are. Their titles would seem to separate them from one another; but they are all united; — their keynote being "The Sanctity of Literature."

MAURICE FRANCIS EGAN.

CONTENTS.

I. SOME WORDS ABOUT CHAUCER.

EVERYTHING concerning the most cheerful, most natural, and most sympathetic of all English poets, Chaucer, has come to be of interest. Whether his name had originally anything to do with footwear or not, or whether it was derived from some small office about the court will perhaps soon be decided by Mr. Skeat; but there is no question that, even in this apparently unimportant matter of philology, the public testifies more than usual concern. The interest in Chaucer is no doubt due to his incomparable charm as a story-teller, the human quality in his poems, and the increase of respect for the English language among English-speaking people.

Chaucer has been examined by the analysts of speech from every point of view, and what the English have left undone the Germans have minutely completed; but there is one thing which most interpreters of Chaucer have failed to grasp, and that is the impossibility of judging the standards of the fourteenth century by those of the nineteenth. As an axiom they are willing to admit that it is illogical to judge the ethical point of view of one age considered from the changed attitude of another. Every expositor of literary history, from Dryden to Lounsbury, from Voltaire to Taine, admits this; but only in the abstract. When it comes to application, both knowledge and intuition

(5)

seem to fail.   This is especially true of nearly
all writers who look at history either through
the telescope supplied by traditional Protestantism or the microscope of "modernity,"
and more especially true of even the cleverest
interpreters of Chaucer, of Montaigne, of
Pascal, of even Sir Thomas More.

In the case of these great men, it is, as a
rule, due not to prejudice, but to that inca-
pacity for projection which no mind but the
synthetically imaginative possesses and to the
hallucination which leads so many writers to
believe that the Catholic in all ages is a slave
to some hidden power, and that his spiritual
life,—of which every detail is supposed to be
dogmatic, — is like a great picture, without
shadow, softness, or perspective.   In Mr. See-
bohm's "Oxford Reformers," the strictures of
Sir Thomas More on the superstition of a
certain friar are used to show that he was
travelling fast towards Lutheranism.   "There
was at Coventry a Franciscan of the unreformed sort," Sir Thomas More writes; "this
man preached in the city, the suburbs of the
neighborhood, and the village about, that
whosoever should say daily the Psalter of the
Blessed Virgin could never be lost.   The
people listened greedily to this easy way of
getting to heaven.   The pastor there, an ex-
cellent and learned man, though he thought
the saying very foolish, said nothing for a time,
thinking that no harm could come from it,
since the people would become more devout to
God from greater devotion to the Blessed

Virgin. But at last he found his flock infected
with such a disease that the very worst were
especially devoted to the rosary for no other
reason than that they promised themselves impunity in everything; for how could they
doubt of heaven, when it was promised to them
with such assurance by so good a man, a friar
direct from Heaven!"

This letter[1] was written in 1519, and Sir
Thomas goes on to tell of his meeting with the
friar, and to repeat his argument against him:

"For, though you may easily find a king
ready to pardon something in an enemy at the
prayers of his mother, yet there is nowhere
one so great a fool as to promulgate a law by
which to encourage the audacity of his subjects
against himself, by a promise of impunity to
traitors, on condition of their paying a certain
homage to his mother. Much was said on
both sides, but I only succeeded in getting
laughed at, while he was extolled."

Sir Thomas adds that he does not intend to
impute crime to any body of religious, "since
the same ground produces herbs both whole-
some and poisonous; nor do I wish to find
fault with those who salute Our Lady, than
which nothing can be more beneficial; but because some trust so much in their devotions
that they draw from them boldness to sin.
May I be held a liar if there are not religious
in certain places who observe silence so
obstinately that at no price could you get them

---

[1] Life of Sir Thomas More. By the Rev. T. E. Bridgett,
of the Congregation of the Most Holy Redeemer.

to whisper in their corridors; but, draw them one foot outside, and they will not hesitate to storm at whoever offends them. There are some who would fear lest the devil should carry them off alive if they made any change in their dress, and who have no fear of heaping up money, of opposing and deposing their abbot. Are there not many who, if they omitted a verse of their office, would think it a crime to be expiated with many tears, and who have not the least scruple to take part in calumnious gossip longer than their longest prayers."

No man familiar with Catholic doctrine and practice, will imagine that Sir Thomas showed a tendency towards the opinions of Luther because of these words or of several similar passages in his defence of his friend Erasmus. And no man, knowing the freedom of Faith, will set down Geoffrey Chaucer either as a Wickliffite or an agnostic because he jests at many things which ought to have an odor of sanctity. One would fancy that authors who assume to write with scientific accuracy might analyze the effects of the teachings of the Catholic Church upon the minds of the people,—and, first, examine as a preparation for this the distinction which the Church makes between the essential and the non-essential. As it is, the doctrines of the Church and the effect of these doctrines on the minds that accept them are the most important, but least understood of all things in modern history.

Sir Thomas More's sympathy was with the parish priest at Coventry, in the sixteenth century; Geoffrey Chaucer's was with the parish priest in general, in the fourteenth century; but even the mistaken "unreformed" friar would not have accused the former of heresy for that only, nor would the Wickliffite have claimed Chaucer as a follower because of his jokes, — coarse to our taste, but merely virile fun from his point of view, — at the expense of the friar; —

"A wantoun and a merry,
A limitour, a full solempné man."

No educated man now believes that Chaucer was a leader in that Wickliffite revolt which preceded the breaking away of England from union with Rome. And few men who have examined the evidence, hold that he was even a follower of Wickliffe. As to Professor Lounsbury's[1] elaborate *apologia* for the scepticism of Chaucer, it proves nothing to the man who can read Chaucer with a subtler understanding. Lovers of the poet are under deep obligation to Professor Lounsbury. To the present time there has been no better book on Chaucer; and its author has further added to his service by putting the testimony as to Chaucer's scepticism at its very strongest point. And this testimony, at its strongest point, is the weakest thing in the book.

[1] Studies in Chaucer, by Thomas R. Lounsbury, Professor of English in the Sheffield Scientific School of Yale University. New York, Harper & Brothers, Vol. III, p. 499.

As a rule, there is not very much gained by trying to settle the personal relations of any human being to God. The real question lies between God and the soul. And the controversies as to whether Shakespere was a practical Catholic or not, or whether Wordsworth had belief in the Immaculate Conception, or whether Rossetti's splendid "Ave" brought him the grace of conversion, seem to be, as Charles Reade puts it, "like the cooking of stale cabbage over farthing candles." It is quite as inutile, and often as malodorous. Beside the illumination of God's mercy, our light is but as a farthing candle. The essence of the poet must be left finally to his Creator. But this is true: "In the very greatest poets, the standard of human law has been absolute sanctity. The key-note of this their theme is usually sounded by them with the utmost reserve and delicacy, especially by Shakespere, but it is there; and every poet — the natural faculties of the poet being pre-supposed—will be great in proportion to the strictness with which, in his moral ideal he follows the counsels of perfection."[1] This is the standard by which the poet must be judged; and judged by their standard, Chaucer is a poet of a very high type. But we logically look into the works of a poet, to form an ultimate opinion, not into his life, on which no man,—not even a judge and jury, with crowds of expert witnesses—can give the final verdict.

---

[1] Religio Poetae: Coventry Patmore. London: George Bell & Sons; p. 84.

It was natural that the Puritans should
claim the first of English poets; it seemed to
strengthen their case to have as the precursor
of their revolt one of the keenest intellects of
the fourteenth century, — a learned man, a
sane-minded man, a man whom all England
esteemed. It was illogical, however, since the
whole spirit and expression of Geoffrey Chaucer, — and the spirit and expression with him
is one,—denies all the fundamentals in which
the Puritans prided themselves. The gaiety
of heart, the love of the natural, the tolerance
for the ailties of humanity, the abounding
charity, the delight in the world as a place of
sunshine, and, if not the best of all possible
worlds, a very good one, — were antagonistic
to every tenet of Puritanism. And these
qualities are characteristic of Chaucer. He
leaves the great questions to be answered by
God. Even when the Pagan Arcite dies,
the Knight says, —

"His spirit changed hous, and wente ther,
As I cam never, I can not tellen wher,
Therefore I stinte[1] I am no divinistre,
Of soules find I not in this registre,
Ne me list[2] thilke opinions to telle
Of hem, though that they writen wher[3] they dwelle.
Arcite is cold, then Mars his soule gie.[4]

On these lines Professor Lounsbury puts the
question: "Can modern agnosticism point to a
denial more emphatic than that made in the
fourteenth century of the belief that there exists for us any assurance of the life that is lived

[1]Stop. [2]Is not my pleasure. [3]Where. [4]Gie—Guide.

beyond the grave!'' To which we might
reply: Could one believe that modern agnosticism should twist such a passage in favor of
itself, if human inconsistency had not already
gone as far by making the wife of Bath a sort
of Protestant Madonna! Theseus, in his dis-
course, near the end of ''The Knight's Tale,''
asks:

> ''Why grucchen we? Why have we heeviness,
> That good Arcite, of chivalry the flour,
> Departed is with duty and honour,
> Out of this foule prison of this lyf?
> Why grucchen here his cosin and his wife
> Of his welfare, that loven him so well?
> Can he them thank? nay, God wot, never a deel.
> That both his soul and eek hem-self offende,
> And yet they mowe[1] hir lustes[2] nat amende.''

Theseus is a Pagan Greek, but his funeral
sermon, paraphrased, is not unknown in pul-
pits which would shake with horror at the
suspicion of agnosticism.

All the world loves a poet; and all the world
loves to seek him in his work, to find the man
whose song delights and uplifts. It sometimes happens that if we chase the meadow
lark we miss the song, and too much seeking
for the man causes us to lose some of the
glamour of the bard. But in his work and
only in his work should we seek him;—for life-
histories, the surface-stories of existence,—are
like the crowing of the cock to Oberon and
Puck, — the signal of chill and grayness and
the vanishing of fantasy.

---

[1]Can. [2]Feelings.

Since the test of the poet is his allegiance, at his best, to high beauty and truth, and he should be valued "in proportion to the strictness with which, in his moral ideal, he follows the counsels of perfection," it is a duty to examine the insinuations which presume that he cannot bear this test.

To us the Church is the spouse of the highest Truth and Beauty. If, therefore, Chaucer had contemned her, we should feel that he had proved himself unworthy of our full regard. If we were obliged to take him as we take Spenser, with regret that he should be forced to be self-consciously Protestant, we would lose the full enjoyment of that *naïveté* which distinguishes him among the other great poets. The Protestantism,—political and politic as it is,—of Spenser is artificial and self-conscious. When he turns Our Lady's face into "a lady's face" in the blazon of a knight's armor, we find that all the magnificence of his crimson vert and azure tapestry will not atone for it. And when Elizabeth is enamelled with allegorical paste, we see at once how impossible Protestantism is from the æsthetic point of view. The Huguenots and the Covenanters may be made to seem heroic by accenting their human qualities, the attributes they have in common with all men of strong will that resist superior force; but their tenets offer no chance for careless gaiety or joy in life.

The more Puritanical Reformers based their claims to Chaucer on works attributed to him which were not his. Charles Cowden Clarke tells us that "the venerable heretic, John Foxe, after alluding to the industry of the Popish clergy in quenching and stamping into the earth those treatises which tended to overthrow the fabric of their hierarchy, considers the presentation of the above works of our poet in the light of an especial Providence." The "above" works were "Jack Upland." "The Plowman's Tale," and "The Testament of Love," which[1] are not Chaucer's, — so that, even if "The Romance of the Rose" be admitted, John Foxe's "special Providence" disappears.

No doubt it would be a convincing thing, if we could show that Geoffrey Chaucer had spent his life in arguing against the Lollards and that he was a determined enemy of Wickliffe; but, unless we invent certain works for him after the manner of Chatterton, and a "special Providence" after the manner of John Foxe, we must be content with the pleasanter thing of accepting him only as a poet and the most intuitive and sympathetic delineator of life the English world of letters possesses, next to Shakespere. On the other hand, those persons who like to think of him as a heretic, must give up their case, since, on examination we find that he was little either of a polemist or a politician. He occupied positions of trust and filled them well, but we do not discern that he pandered to any political party in order to enjoy either his positions or his pensions. If he did, there is no evidence of it in his works,

---

[1] See Lounsbury, Vol. II, p. 4.

or in any other written record yet discovered.
The prose "Parson's Tale" seems to be essentially sound, whether it be entirely the composi-
tion of Chaucer or not. It seems to have been
added to make amends for those "endytinges
of vanities" which have so much endeared him
to the world, but which he retracts towards
the end of his life in a manner which is anything but sceptical. At the same time, it
must be admitted that, as literature, neither
the "Parson's Tale" nor the "Retraccion" has
any interest whatever. The "Parson's Tale"
may be a good sermon, from the point of view
of moral theology on the seven deadly sins
and the "Retraccion" is the expression of a
devout mind which fears the effect of scandal
and no doubt regrets the "gyltes" for which
it is so contrite. And the "Reeve's" and
"Miller's Tale" ought indeed to be followed
by some beating of the breast.[1]

If the advocates for Chaucer's "Lollardism"
will drop their contention and the pleaders for
his scepticism admit that a man may be averse
to superstition and yet be a good Catholic, I,
for my part, am quite willing to let Chaucer
be judged as a poet, not as an apostle or
preacher of any sort. It would give me a
great pang to have to regard Chaucer as a
Wickliffite, but it would be even more painful
if all his works had been as unexceptionable
and dull as the "Parson's Tale," which is
utterly lacking in poetical value, and yet which
might have been preached by the best of regu-

[1] See Lounsbury, Vol. II, p. 4.

lars or seculars.   As a political writer, on either
side, he would have ceased to be poetical.   Let
us have him as he is, — a son of the Church,
amused rather than shocked by laxities in dis-
cipline; not loth to point them out, inclined to
take part against the friars and to use the stock
jokes on his side; broad in his speech, not
vexed by modern ideas of purity, given to a
jesting license, but never intrinsically licenti-
ous.   He called a spade a spade; and, if the
spade was muddy, he made no attempt to pretend that it was clean.

Nobody, except a purblind special pleader
here and there, has ever denied that Sir
Thomas More, — not so long ago pronounced
blessed, — was a most devout Catholic.   And
yet he did not hesitate to denounce superstition when he thought he saw it or to find fault
with abuses similar to some of them which
Chaucer rather cheerfully chronicles.   Not
that Chaucer ever apologizes for evil or blurs
the line that divides right from wrong.   He is
too safe in faith and the morality that flows
from faith for that; he is so safe, in fact, that
he can afford to take liberties.   More would
have been the first to admit that Erasmus'
"Praise of Folly," which seemed innocuous
when men were united in the essentials of belief, had become dangerous when a thousand
attacks on these essentials were made; and, in
1532, More did admit this in a letter to Erasmus.   Similarly Chaucer must be judged in
the light of his times.   The reader who would
condemn his poems because of his jests at

abuses, which certainly did exist, but which
were no more general than that all Irishmen
have pug noses or that all mothers-in-law are
tyrants, is as narrow-minded as that other,
who, because Chaucer jeered at the friars and
smiled at the worldly caprices of the charming
Lady Abbess, holds that he was as iconoclastic
as Wickliffe, and denied the spiritual power of
the Church. The stock Irishman and the
stock mother-in-law of the "comic" papers
hold to-day the place which the gluttonous
friar, the avaricious monk, and the betrayed
husband have in the vulgar annals of the fourteenth century. If Chaucer lived to-day—if,
Walter Savage Landor[1] or Marion Crawford[2]
were real magicians and could have brought
him into our century,—he would no doubt be
astonished to find himself assumed by pious
Catholics as a defender of the Church, claimed
by the Protestant as a splendid heretic and by
the agnostic as a sceptic. Alive, he would
find it as hard to understand the nineteenth
century point of view as we find it to tolerate
a century which outraged many of those con-
ventionalities that we have accepted as principles. A satirical turn of mind, like a renown
for repartee, may carry a man too far. But
because Chaucer gave his characters every
opportunity for laughing at false relics, it does
not follow that he had no reverence for the
true. England, as he pictures it, with all its
merriment, — not always an ideal or innocent
merriment, by any means, — was evidently in

---

[1] Imaginary Conversations. [2] With the Immortals.

training for the woe to come in the time of
Henry VIII.   The evil lay in him who pur-
veyed falsehood and traded in the vestibules of
the sanctuary, not in him whose wit flashed upon
such treachery.   Chaucer evidently felt that
the human side of the Church was fair material
for him; but no writer has ever shown a finer
conception of the spiritual side of our priest-
hood than he, in the famous description of the
good pastor, in the prologue to the "Canter-
bury Tales":

"A better priest, I trowe, that nowhere noon is."[1]

"The Wife of Bath's Tale" is held up as
one of the poet's attacks on what some com-
mentators seem to believe to be a dogma of the
Church,—the celibacy of the clergy.   Professor
Lounsbury says:—"There can be no question
as to the poet's position in this matter.[2]   His
contempt for the doctrine, and the reasons
advanced in its favor, is scarcely ever dis-
guised.   The confounding of celibacy with
chastity excites his scorn.   It is hardly necessary to observe that at such a period the expression of sentiments of this kind is not made
the ostensible, or even prominent, motive for
producing the work.   Nor would these sentiments be put forth by Chaucer in his own
person or in that of any serious character.   It
was not accident that led to the selection of
the speaker.   It was no fondness for coarseness for coarseness' sake that dictated the tone

---

[1] Skeat: Complete Edition.   Macmillan.
[2] Studies in Chaucer, Vol. II, p. 525.

which is frequently found in the poem. It is in the mouth of one like the sensual, shrewd, and worldly wife of Bath, who boasts that she has already had five husbands, and is ready to welcome the sixth whenever he presents himself that an attack upon celibacy could be safely placed."

Now the plain-spoken wife of Bath is not a person whom one would like to meet in a modern drawing-room, at an afternoon tea, unless one was sure that she were unaccompanied by an interpreter of Middle English; for she is certainly very frank; but her talk is much less intrinsically coarse than a great deal of modern after-dinner conversation, founded on many French and some English novels. It is surprising that Professor Lounsbury should tell us that Chaucer did not make her "coarse" for the sake of "coarseness." He might just as well apologize for St. James or St. Augustine or St. Chrysostom, whose utterances, if made in a pulpit to-day, to any well-dressed congregation within the bounds of the English speech, would be received with amazement. "If we go back," says Coventry Patmore, "to those first ages of Christianity—which modern good people who know nothing about them, regard with such reverence — we shall find that the greatest and purest of the 'Fathers of the Church' were in the practice of addressing their flocks with an outspokenness which is not surpassed even by the ancient expounders of the Eleusinian and Bacchic mysteries, or, for that matter, by the Bible

itself.[1] St. Augustine, for example, in the
City of God and elsewhere, says things fit to
throw decent people into convulsions; and
nowhere, in ancient Christian writings, do we
find ignorance regarded as even a part, much
less the whole of innocence." The wife of
Bath was of her time; Chaucer did not make
her; she existed, and he drew her as she was,
with a humor, a knowledge of character, and
a delight in his picture which distinguishes
him as an artist. In Chaucer's eyes she was
a very respectable woman; she had a "past"
and a bad temper; the first, Chaucer, like a
gentleman, treats delicately; the second, he
illustrates, —

> [2] "In all the parish, wife ne there was none,
> That to the off'ring before her shouldè gone,
> And, if there did, certain so wroth was she
> That she was out of allè charity.
> Her coverchiefs weren full fine of ground ;
> I durstè swear they weigheden a pound
> That on the Sunday were upon her head :
> Her hosen weren of fine scarlet red,
> Full strait y tied and shoes full moist and new;
> Bold was her face, and fair and red of hew."

She had made pilgrimages; she knew the
world; and, in the "Prologue"[3] to her story,
she remarks:

---

[1] Religio Poetae, p. 102.

[2] Riches of Chaucer: Charles Cowden Clarke (Expurgated
edition).

[3] Skeat.

"Experience, though noon auctoritee
Were in this world, were right y-nough to me,
To speak of wo that is in mariage ;
For, lordinges, since I twelf yeer was of age,
Thonked be God that is eterne on lyve,
Husbands at churchè-dore I have had five ;
For I so oftè have y-wedded be,
And alle were worthy men in hir degree."

She has heard the Scriptures preached, and
a scruple—very slight—has been raised by the
assertion,

"That sith Crist ne wentè never but onis
To wedding in the Cane of Galilee,
That by the same ensample taught he me
That I ne sholdè wedded be but once."

She admits, not with contempt, as Professor
Lounsbury suggests, but with entire simplicity,
that —

——a lord in his household,
He hath nat every vessel al of gold ;
Somme been of tree, and doon hir lord servyse,
God clepeth folk to Him in sondry wyse,
And everich hath of God a propre yiftè,
Som this, som that—as Him lyketh shifte.
Virginitee is great perfeccioun,
And contiuence eek with devocioun."

If Chaucer, in the second half of the fourteenth century, had taken upon himself the
mission of combating St. Paul, St. Jerome,
and the general voice of the Church on this
counsel of perfection, the "Wife of Bath's
Tale" might have been of greater comfort to
Henry VIII., who, in his own showing, had

certain scruples, too; but it would not be the recital of a man of genius, who was consequently a man of insight, — of a story-teller who drew life and character as he saw it, with humor and pathos. And these, joined with moral perception, make that quality which, in Montaigne and Thackeray, some call "cynicism."

A man, bred in Protestantism, cannot, unless he has almost miraculous perception, understand the point of view of the Catholic of the fourteenth century; and, I admit, it is very difficult for a Catholic, tinged with the false asceticism of Protestantism, — as we all are, more or less,—to condone that old-time plain-speaking which goes to the root of things without concealment. And yet Chaucer had a certain reserve and modesty by which moderns might profit. His persons accept the eternal varieties; there is no question of the spiritual authority of the Church, no doubt as to the Trinity; the Godhead of Christ and His attributes are lovingly spoken of,—there are no sneers at the Sacrament of Penance and the Eucharist. In Chaucer's time, or even in Sir Thomas More's, if a man could not distinguish the precious wine of God from the earthen vessel that held it, he was accounted a fool. This distinction was often made with a vengeance. Whether it was expedient or not is not now the question. Whether the earthen vessel could be roughly touched without injury to the treasure it held, is another question. The Continental and English peoples thought it could, — the

Irish were of a different opinion or of a different temperament.

The "merry words of the host to the monk" in the "Monk's Prologue" are quoted frequently in support of Chaucer's "reforming" proclivities. This wise, humorous, keen and sympathetic observer of humanity, it is said, was ahead of his time; he foresaw that, if the best men entered the Church and bound themselves to celibacy, the English race, indeed all the races of the earth, must dwindle into feeble folk. It was not only the lessening of the physique he feared, but the lessening of the intellect of the future. If the Church, — the pestilant cormorant of John Foxe and Bunyon, — seized the most comely, the wisest, surely the heretics were benefactors of the world, when they declared that all vows of celibacy were cursed of God! It is this view that many serious-minded persons, determined to make the poet polemical, have read into the "Monk's Prologue." The "tale of Melibee" is finished, and the host, whose language is "plain," cries out that he wishes he had a patient wife.

> "I had lever than a barel of ale
> That goode lief my wyf hadde herd this tale!
> For she nis nothing of swich pacience
> As was this Melibeus wfe Prudence."

According to his further account, the lady of his thoughts is a rather difficult person. It becomes evident that, supposing the monasteries have assumed nearly all the strong-limbed and strong-minded men, the convents

have not succeeded in securing all the valiant
women. If, for instance, as the host pro-
claims, a neighbor jostles his wife at church
or does not salute her, she

> ——"cryeth false coward, wreek thy wyf.
> By *corpus bones!* I wol have thy knyf,
> And thou shalt have my distaff and go spinnè !
> Fro day to night right thus she wol beginnè ;—
> 'Allas,' she saith, 'that ever I was shape,
> To wed a milksop or a coward ape,
> That will be overlad with every wight.
> Though darst not stonden by thy wyves right !"

The host prophesies that he will be forced
to murder by this belligerent wife of his, and
then turns to the monk, audibly regretting
that such a fine man of religion is not married.
After his description of the woes of married
life, there is an ironical humor in this regret
which the serious-minded polemist can not
see. It is logical enough that, reflecting on
the masterful strength of the lady hostess, he
sighs to consider the brawn and sinew of the
monk, who might have withstood her, "so big
in armes." It is not logical, under the circum-
stances, that he should commend marriage to
the guest, "but," he says:—

> ——and I were pope
> That only thou but every mighty man,
> Thogh he were shorn ful hye upon the pan
> Should have a wyf; for all the world is lorn
> Religioun hath take up al the corn
> Oftreding, and we borel men ben shrimpes !
> Of feble trees their comen wretched imps.' "

The host here makes a compliment perhaps
unconsciously to the strictness with which the
monks kept their vows,—a compliment which
is generally overlooked by interpreters who
would turn the lark-like poems of Chaucer into "problem" essays. The host suddenly
drops into a tone of banter quite in his own
manner, for which he apologizes, as well he
might.—

> "But be not wrooth, my Lord, for that I pleye;
> Ful oft in game a sooth I have herd seye.
> 'This worthy monk took al in pacience.'"

This monk, "worthy," as Chaucer names
him, was a "manly man," given to hunting
and not to study; not a recluse or a hard
worker, or a strict follower of the rule of St.
Benedict, but a believer in the newer and more
worldly ways, in which Chaucer seems to
sympathize with him. He was a "fair prelate,"
splendid in the adornments of himself and his
hounds, his fur-trimmed sleeves and his berry-
brown palfrey, his well-colored face and his
curious gold pin give Chaucer as much pleasure
as the tints in a cardinal's robe give Vibert or
the rain drops on a soldier's helmet, Detaille.
There is a place for this dignified and splendid
monk in the pleasant world as for the hard-
working parson and the clerk of Oxenford.
Even the friar, who would have been declared
accursed by St. Francis d' Assisi, finds ironical
tolerance with Chaucer,

> "And in his harping, when that he had sung,
> His eyen twinkled in his head aright
> As do the starres on a frosty night."

He makes a picture; he will tell his story in the soft April weather, by the Thames. It is no time or place for denunciation, — God will give every man his desert in good time. And Geoffrey Chaucer is not Hamlet, born to set the world right.

Let us take him as he was, and let us not ask that he be other than he was. He was not Dante, eagle-like, but bitter and brooding. He did not hate both the sin and the sinner, after the manner of the great Florentine. He did not penetrate to Hell or soar to Heaven. Earth, — the daisied earth, where the little birds sang, and gay voices joined with them,— was beloved of him. Nothing natural was alien to him; he was a humanist, but not a Hedonist,—in love with life, but not an Epicurean. That beneath him was the sure rock of eternal truth he never seems to have doubted. Safe and certain, like Sir Thomas More, his later brother, with whose humor he had so much in common, he could let his fancy play with no thought of danger. His geniality, his acuteness in knowledge of the foibles of humanity, his optimism, his power of picturing, his grace and immortal freshness make him beloved of the world. He borrowed his stories as Shakespere did; he was the first to English them, and they are his, whether Dante or Petrarch or Boccaccio or old folks by the fire told them before or not. On the verdant ground of the spring time of a nation he planted a garden of perennial beauty. On the gray walls of a gloomy palace, — half-Saxon mead hall, half-feudal castle,—he hung a tapestry, filled with the crimson of love and the azure of hope. He waved his wand, and henceforth England was called "merrie." His gaiety had the *naïveté* of a child, — of a child who does not doubt and who does not fear. It came from a heart that knew the beauty of Truth. All those high human qualities, which Christianity illuminates but does not create, were beloved of him. As in the cathedral carvings of his time, we find in his work strange things which modern taste, more delicate, rejects. Like all men of genius, he was of his time, but not of the worst of it. That he hated the faith that conserved beauty in England we may as soon believe as that Shakespere would have torn the door from the tabernacle of his own church at Stratford, or blotted the "requiescat" from a neighbor's tomb. Polemist he was not; crusader he was not; but what he was, in heart, we can guess from his prayer—

> "Glorious mayde and moder, which that never[1]
> Were bitter, neither in erthe nor in see,
> But ful of swetnesse and of mercy ever,
> Help that my fader be not wroth with me."

---

[1] A. B. C. Skeat.

II. ON THE TEACHING OF ENGLISH.

THE teaching of the English language and literature is at present largely experimental. So composite is the language and so varied the literature, that men differ widely even as to the manner of approaching them for the purpose of serious study. It is only of late—and mostly here in the United States — that the literature, apart from the language, has come to be looked on as worthy of earnest consideration.

In Italy, even foolish men would have cried shame had Dante been left by the schools and universities to the mercy of the first reader who should take up the Divine Comedy. To have ignored the greatest of all poets in the scheme of education would have seemed monstrous. To have reduced the most spiritual of all poems, except Isaias and Job and the Apocalypse, to a mere exercise in philology would have caused the driest-minded of the Italians to laugh. Similarly, the Germans, when they regard our methods of instruction at all, wonder why we seem to look on a vital principle in our natural life with such little interest. The literature of a country is its song of battle and its hymn of immortality. It sends the blood to the heart and out again; it is a part of life. It is not an accomplishment; in a certain sense, it is the science of life,—for as Professor Moulton, of the University of

(28)

Chicago, has recently pointed out, — the poet and the novelist, like the modern physicist, choose the qualities of life and set them in motion before us. Dante, for instance, concretes the supernatural, and we see the spiritual life of man humanized, brought to us, as the physicist brings the very essence of the frost and the heat and the impalpable forces of the air within the knowledge of the growing child. Dante did for philosophy what Plato had attempted in his "Symposium," and for theology what nobody had the genius to do until he, with sublime self-confidence, began to write. The Divine Comedy of Dante is to *scientia* what modern laboratory work is to modern science. The Germans understand this better than we do, and, in the earliest schools for their children, they assume that literature,—which is, at the same time, universal and personal,—ought to be correlated with the other studies that go to make the man and the citizen. The growth of the literary feeling is gradual; it is a part of life — of every-day life. A man or woman of education in Germany does not suddenly awaken to the fact of the existence of literature and clutch at it as a part of culture. There is among the Germans no frantic efforts to grasp the "Heliand," or the "Song of Roland," or Marlowe's versification, or Sordello as a thing exotic, — apart and special from its fecundating stream of literature. The German specialists, like Herr Delius, do not disregard the spirit of literature, however wedded to the letter they may be. It is certain, at least, that whatever attitude they may take towards the literature of other peoples, they are heart to heart with their own. They do not look on the lightest lyric of Goethe as altogether trivial; nor do they mentally rush at his Alpine heights without having acquired that surety of balance which comes of having laboriously ascended the rocks below. This can not be said of English-speaking people,—and it may be said less of Americans even than of the English themselves. The road to university work in English literature is, consequently, neither wide nor unimpeded.

There are two sides from which learners approach the study of English — from the philological side and from the philosophical side — we may almost say, with Matthew Arnold, from the ethical side. The philologist seems at times to underrate the necessity of interpretation or exposition; he believes in "words, words, words," without the accent of scorn which Hamlet used in speaking to Polonius. He is unduly reverent to the least motion of evolution in the word and somewhat contemptuous of the changes of the thought. Words are only attempts to speak what is unspeakable until genius wrenches them to its purpose. Yet words are history. The Elgin marbles are no more important to the archæologist than the verbal form "are" is to the philologist; and the Pelasgic survivals in Greek are as epoch-making to him as the discoveries at Troy. Words, after all, are only symbols of the volatile essence of life; the thoughts, the emotions, the moods, which caught forever in the right phrase, are literature. The inordinate preponderance of mere philology in the university study of English has really as a basis the fear that literature, apart from its garb of words, cannot give a concrete form for examinations for honors.

The rigid pedagogue shrinks from things of taste; they are subtle and undefined; they are gaseous, more than gaseous, or less. You cannot catch them in a glass globe or tabulate them. What the rhetoricians have said of the classics he may accept, but no literature, in his estimation, has vitality until it is dead. He genuflects to Homer and bows to Virgil; he is respectful to Anacreon and Horace; they can be made subjects for examinations. Even the historical value of words is held by him to be less than their worth as parts of the letter. Consequently, it is often the case that one finds a learned man, sympathetic only for words, who condescends to smile at all talk about the spiritual value of literature in the higher education, who scorns its scientific treatment, who longs for a heaven in which he might give the same attention to the vocative case which, in this life, he had already given to the dative!

Shakespere is not actually great to every man who calls himself educated and cultivated; nor is Dante. There are men who yawn over Job and rave about that sublime introduction to "Faust," which Goethe has appropriated from Job. These men need to be illuminated; for they accept things blindly; they have eyes,

but they have not been taught to see. It is
the vocation of the teacher of English literature to show them how to see. If Shakespere
is great, there must be reasons for his greatness—reasons which only the thoughtless will
tell us can be left to intuition. The scientific
method, if it be worth anything, ought to be
capable of application to the works of a man
who is held by the human race to be one of
its glories.

Dante is nothing to many men of special
training in colleges and universities, because
he has never been interpreted to them. We
Catholics, who accept the Sacred Books only
as the Church gives them to us, ought certainly
to see that the word of genius is as "caviare
to the general" until reverently and lucidly
exposed.

There is a feeling among us Americans that
every man who votes is able to understand
anything symbolized by English words. To
read, with us, means to understand. To admit
that anything in English letters is beyond our
capacity is un-American and un-English. If
the careless tyro, fed on newspapers, finds
Newman or Tennyson or Browning incom-
prehensible, it is the writer who is obscure!
In China they are more civilized than this.

It is almost heresy to say that there is a
lapse in a man's educational training if he cannot understand Tennyson's "Two Voices" or
Patmore's "Ode to the Body." The beauty
and meaning of these poems are hidden to ten
thousand men out of every ten thousand and

one, because their minds and hearts have not
been educated to discover them. In our depths
we have a tradition that, while reading and
writing do not come by nature, the power of
perceiving the beauty of works which God
takes thousands of years to formulate is a
faculty which requires neither systematic education nor cultivation;—and that literature is
valuable as a kind of decoration to more solid
things.

The French long ago set the example by
taking their literature as seriously as the
Greeks. A Frenchman may differ from
another Frenchman on almost every subject,
but when it is a matter of literary judgment of
the classics of his own country you will find
harmony. He may hate Voltaire's object,
which was to scorn and degrade, but he will
admire those qualities of style which made
Voltaire so dangerous. And just as we find
the old and the new *régimes* meeting in Paris
in the museum of national relics in the house
of Madame de Sévigné, we observe that literature, the approved litreature of France, is
common ground. After all, the French are
the most artistic of peoples; they are the
modern Greeks; love of art with them is
virtue followed by a black shadow of vice;
there are those among them who have
no love for St. Genevieve, except when their
first woman patriot is portrayed by Puvis de
Chavannes. So fine is their art in literature
that they have almost persuaded the world of
the greatness of their modern poets. There is

no question that their prose is the most exquisite prose written in our time. There are pages of Bossuet and Pascal, of Fénelon and Voltaire, of Chateaubriand and Gautier which seem to have exhausted all the capabilities of the written phrase. These pages are not the result of racial temperament. They are the outcome of serious study of the art of personal expression, subjected to certain canons discovered through intense devotion to the production of style. No cultivated Frenchman affects to hold the great authors of his nation lightly, or as unworthy of strenuous attention and careful study. In the earlier schools his memory has been filled with beautiful passages from them. The French teachers are not afraid of memory tasks in literature, because they know how to make them lead to something better. Nearly every French schoolboy knows by heart splendid things from the great authors, and, out of ten schoolboys, I found not long ago that eight knew by heart the whole of Malherbe's "Consolation á M. Perrier," the other two substituting for this minor poem some verses from Coppée and the "Connais tu le pays," translated from Goethe. I found that they had been taught to believe that the study of their literature was as important as that of Latin and Euclid.

With us it has been different. We have only recently begun to look on the study of English, — excepting, of course, the rudimentary grammar and philology, — as of any real importance. We are still afraid of the

"cram" in our preparatory schools; it is to be
hoped that the words Professor Dowden says
in favor of the earlier "cram," in his "New
Studies in Literature," may turn the advocates
of everything inductive to that system of mem-
ory-work which has had so much to do with the
unexampled success of the Jesuits in the teaching of Latin to the young.   Miss Austin, in the
beginning of this century, complains of the
Philistine point of view of the English towards
the novel, and with gentle sarcasm alludes to
the "elegant extracts," which, arranged by
some dullard, were accepted by teachers as the
commencement and the end of English literature.   When the English interpreted the phrase
"belles-lettres" into "polite learning," they
did literature a bad turn, for it has taken them
a good many years to discover that anything
"polite" can be worth serious attention.   Addi-
son might have passed under this title, but
how Swift could ever have been signalized by
it is beyond comprehension; — and it is lucky
it went out of fashion before Carlyle made his
mark.   At last one of the greatest universities
in the world, Oxford, has begun a school of
English,—only begun it!   And there are some
among her dons and disciples who fear that
the term "polite learning" or "belles-lettres,"
may be thrown at them and detract from the
dignity of a faculty that every year condescends
to offer a prize for a poem in English.

The action,—or reaction,—against the ultra-
conservative view of English literature is
almost too violent.   It has taken the form of a

protest against philology and memory work,—
in forgetfulness of the truth that the spirit of
the text lies hidden until the letter is mastered.
There is something humorous in the flight of
an American teacher of English from mere
philology in his own country to Oxford and
Cambridge, and from thence, in despair, to
Leipsic or Freiburg. If he should import
Fritz Reuter's books to study the modern
development of the Anglo-Saxon, or dig into
Platt-Deutsch, as some men study modern
Greek after Homer and Theocritus, there
would be more reason in his mission. But,
although in the teaching of English neither
the Anglo-Saxon nor the root languages of
the Anglo-Saxon, nor the composite tongues
that make up our language can be neglected,
the means of showing the student how to gain
perspective and sympathy and insight in our
literature are to be found at home. The perspective must be historical,—a vista of epochs;
the sympathy genuine and made concurrent
with the steps of taste by the study of a few
great works, and the insight secured by research into the forces that produce these great
works. Goethe had his effect on Sir Walter
Scott, and Rousseau affected Goethe; — but,
beyond this, there was something in the air
that colored the spirit of Sir Walter, roman-
tical and unseen influences that perpetuated
the sentimental feeling of Prévost's "Manon
Lescaut" and "The New Héloïse" in Sterne,
in "The Sorrows of Werther," and in "Paul
and Virginia." To trace this influence, to

analyze it, to make it clear through its development in the letters, the memoirs, the novels,
the essays of the time, is one of the first duties
of the teacher of literature. Whether literature
be the experimental science of life or not, —
whether poetry offer a standard of living or
not, — this thing is true: that literature is as
much the reflector of life in all times as archi-
tecture was of certain phases of life.

To speak more clearly on this matter of com-
paring literature, great artists, not artists of
equal greatness, have, in three pictures, shown
with terrible force the depths to which un-
bridled sensuousness may lead men. These
artists are Rubens, in the brutal "Kermesse,"
Van Steen, in his "Feast in the Flemish Inn,"
and Couture, in his picture of the orgy among
the Romans in their decadence. Their pictures
are good when studied alone, but more useful,
spiritually and artistically, when studied together. Ruben's manner did not influence
Couture, but Couture must have seen the
"Kermesse" and "The Feast," and the same
spirit dominates all three. Prévost without
his time, Sterne without Rousseau, Shakespere
without Marlowe, Racine without Seneca, Pope
without Boileau, Tennyson without Theocritus
and Byron, are only half understood. The
reaction in favor of the grave consideration of
English literature in university courses has
naturally alarmed men who want visible signs
in the shape of examination results as the
evidence for honors. And the declaration of
other men who belong strictly to the school of

interpretative literature, that examinations are
useless, adds to this alarm. Professor Moulton, one of the pioneers in the study of English
literature from the interpretative side, does
not go so far. If he were technical, it would
be no more than one would expect from a
Cambridge man; but he, like Professor Dowden, gives the examination its just place, and
holds that scholarship in English letters may
be adequately shown without an exaggerated
emphasis on mere philology. At Cambridge
the English tripos is almost entirely a philological test. At Oxford, the beginning of the
school of English is a sign that Oxford will,
henceforth, treat our language as it has hitherto
treated Greek, — for the beauty beneath the
visible words. And it deserves such treatment.
An eminent authority at Harvard was quoted
some time ago as having said that a man might
be graduated to-day from a university without
the knowledge of any language but his own.
A knowledge of English and the power of
using it requires a sufficient acquaintance with
the tongues that make our language. In the
years that precede the university course, the
natural sciences ought to form part of the preparation. They are as necessary as the power
to analyze good prose. If the study of the
physics merely give the man of letters breadth
and correctness in his metaphors, it will have
served its purpose. In truth, no culture can
be too high or too deep for the man who wants
to bring his best and to get the best from the
superb literature which we call English, but

which contains the finest thought of all nations;
for art, like nature

"Give us what we bring;
Not more, nor any less."

The interpretative school holds that the real
ancestors of Tennyson and Newman, Aubrey
de Vere and Walter Savage Landor, Irving
and Hawthorne, were the Greeks and the
Latins, the French and the Italians, and that
if Beowulf and Caedmon's poems are valuable
historically, they have been without permanent
effect either on the spirit or the letter of
English. Professor Moulton claims that the
poet and the novelist are the scientists of our
life. Like the physicist, they draw from the
air and the clouds and the earth such elements
as they need to show men truth about themselves and their race.

"The poet and the novelist," he says, "can
go far beyond this"—the survey of what has
actually happened—"they can reach the very
heart of things by contriving human experiments; setting up, however artificially, the
exact conditions and surroundings that will
give a vital clearness to their truth. Physical
science stood still for ages while its method
was limited to actual observation of nature; it
commenced its rapid advance when modern
times invented the idea of experiment."

M. Zola bolsters up a bad practice by a
bolder theory than this, in his apologia, "The
Experimental Novel." Professor Moulton has
no bad practice to excuse; he is right, and it

is a pity that in few courses of university
English is the novel as a factor in life so seriously taken into the scheme of education, as
at Yale by Prof. William Lyon Phelps. We
Catholics ought to advance towards this, for
we are always quick to see the dangers of a
false philosophy taught alluringly.

When from the primary school literature is
made a part of life and correlated with other
studies, the college student will have been prepared to look at it reverently, and accept the
high claims of a language which, a lute in
Chaucer's hands, became an organ in Milton's,
to which fifty later writers have each added a
new note. The German child learns many
lessons from Schiller's "Bell"; he connects
the making of the bell with his early course of
familiar science. Our little boys read a chapter
out of "Callista" or a lay of Macaulay's as if
it had no connection at all with any other
study. When the pupil shall have been
adequately prepared,—and our reasons for this
preparation are entirely practical, — the work
of the teacher in the higher departments will
be much more easily formulated. He will be
able, then, to begin to widen the perspective
already given, to lead his students to study
one great work from every point of view, and
all the other great works that have influenced
it. And thus the one great work will be a
nucleus for the highest culture, and when the
student has mastered it, he will hold in his
breast the germ of all great things. Any
system of education that does not help the

student to know the truth about himself is inadequate. "To have lived to be famous and to die not knowing oneself is to have failed," Seneca says.

As things are, the teacher of English literature must be prepared to make a comparative course in English. Our language is capable of expressing the sublimity and beauty of the masterpieces. The form of the lyric is untranslatable. But the spirit of Homer is in Chapman's English and in Lord Derby's English, and Dante lives through Cary and Longfellow. To read "The Comedy of Errors" without Plautus, or "Two Gentlemen of Verona" without Lope de Vega and Molière, is to be half informed. And the comparisons must be made in English to be effective; otherwise, they become a mere juggling with names. If the student is prepared to go to the Greek of the Œdipus after he has read "King Lear" or to the Spanish of Calderon when he has finished the "Paradise Lost," or to the "Orlando" of Ariosto when the last fairy echo of Spenser has died away, so much the better. But if he cannot, he will find solace in the English translations. "And," says Professor Dowden "if English literature be connected in our college and university courses with either Greek or Latin or French or German literature, the thoughtful student can hardly fail to be aroused by his comparative studies to consider questions which demand an answer in philosophy." And where can these be better answered than in a Catholic university?

Brunetière, in his "New Essays on Literature,"[1] expresses a truth which ought to make the mere philologist, who sees in English study only a subject for the traditional examination, pause. The French language, Brunetière says, will live because of the creations of Corneille and Racine, and the thoughts of Bossuet and Montesquieu. "L'unique danger que je rédouterais, ce serait donc que notre langue, mal informée de sa propre fortune, en vint à méconnaitre un jour les vraies raisons de son universalité."

It is not the Scandinavian strength of our language, or the Saxon directness, or the Norman copiousness, or the power and plasticity it has borrowed from everywhere that makes it so splendid; but the spirit inarticulate without it, and the marks of the masters who have forced it to speak with the Italian music of "Lycidas" and the Greek fineness of "The Idea of a University."

---

[1] Nouveaux Essais sur la Littérature Contemporaine: 1895.

III. THE SANCTITY OF LITERATURE.

IN the three dialogues of a certain Valla — a
Neo-Pagan of the early Renaissance, now
almost forgotten — the doctrine that pleasure
is the end of life is seductively set forth. All
forms of art, — poetry, painting, sculpture,
music, — are merely for the pleasure of the
moment; and Valla, in the form of one of his
talkers, Beccadelli, sneers at the severer arguments of another personage of the dialogue,
Niccolò Niccoli. Valla is dead, and when he
died there were friends of his who preferred to
say, in good classical Latin, that he had gone
to his gods rather than mar their phrase by
the later Christian expression;—Valla is gone;
who knows whither? — yet his desire and the
desire of his Beccadelli still is with many of
our time. Beccadelli, a real person who denied
Christianity when he wrote "Hermaphroditus," and was not a mere figment of Valla's
brain on which to hang words in the dialogue
"On Pleasure," did his best, when the world
most needed high ideals, to tear from literature the crown and robe of sanctity and to
clothe her in the yellow garb of the abandoned.
And there were many like him. Boccacio
tried it— and repented too late for succeeding
generations to profit by his repentance. The
poison which he put into the most exquisite
prose still attracts and still kills. The world
of art is full of men who, in the name of art,

(43)

defend and follow him. "Thou, Nature, art
my goddess" is their formula. And "art for
art's sake" they add to this.

But nature has nothing the soul of man does
not take to it, — nothing of value to his soul.
And art without aspiration breaks when the
heart rests against it as the white lilac on which
Maurice de Guérin, trusting Nature, leaned.
Art, whose end is not beyond this life, is
beautiful and blind, — the slave of the de-
praved; her sanctity and dignity are gone; her
beauty perverted. Both nature and art fail as
helpers and consolers when they begin and
end with themselves. The hymn to nature
ends with a nocturne to Pan, like Carducci's
ode to Satan. To worship nature is to fall
below nature; to praise pleasure as the end of
art, as expressed in any fine poem, is to burn
incense to the old gods who fled when the
Galilean was crucified.

All art must have an object, and this object
will be, except where the art is a mere copy of
things that seem to have no soul, either God
or Satan, Christ or Pan. Notice that the
votaries of "nature as it is," the realists who
claim merely to copy, and the believers in "art
for art's sake" always teach, as well as those
who claim that art, in its highest form—literature—exists only for pleasure. M. Zola, who
pretends only to be natural, who calls himself
a naturalist, suddenly becomes a teacher of
experimental science. He frankly tells us
that his novel is a dissecting-room and his
people corpses, ulcerous, foul, with the soul

gone. He can not find the soul, and the body has no holiness for him; he teaches how vile life is, and teaches it with passion; and yet he began merely as a copyist of nature. And so Catullus, the Pagan, and Beccadelli, of the "Hermaphroditus," and Swinburne, of the "Songs Before Sunrise," teach that pleasure is the object of life, and that when the raptures of passion and the roses of desire are dead, there is no life. Literature, highest when most artistic, may be dragged to the earth, cast to the swine, but it will always be for God or against Him. And the greatest literature is called divine, because it is with Him. It is sacred.

The Word of God has the sublimest of all epics, — Job; the sweetest of pastoral poems, Ruth; the most glowing of soul-songs in the Psalms of David, the most magnificent of poem-pictures in the Apocalypse. These were directly inspired by God; they were not of men. They are above the literature of men, and yet they are literature, since God spoke through men, and they are personal.

Literature reflects life; life without ideals is death. Literature,—all fine art, in truth,—is an expression of the instinct of immortality. The fern in the damp and dark cranny grows towards the light; the creature grows towards its God. The man longs to get beyond himself. In his winter room, by his smouldering fire, among his rags, he dreamed that he was a prince, — the equal of the noble who yesterday kicked him from his path. And the tale

grew; he did wonderful things and he became
a hero; he was immortal, for the human being
longs to be immortal. The first Christmas
came; a more wondrous story was sung by
the angels; the man awoke to find himself immortal; the ladder of sleep had led higher than
he knew; he was veritably the son of a King.
And so all myths touch truth somewhere;
"fairy tales are the dreams of the poor;" they
are simple expressions of the longing for life
beyond this; and the fairies of our childhood
need only wings to be angels.

Literature tells us the hopes of a nation
and the hope of him who writes; it is national;
it is personal; it tells not only the hopes, but
the ideals; and for this reason it becomes
history. He who goes to Homer for mere
facts wastes his time, — and yet Homer with-
draws the curtain from the beginning of
Greece. And from his myths, — facts made
grandiose by the desire of men to be greater
than themselves, — facts immortalized, — history for Greece begins. Who can read the
Iliad and forget the Unseen, the Judge and
the tribunal beyond this life? The sense of
religion fails in no part of it. There is the
roar of battle and the conflict of wills and the
war of right and wrong and the swell of the
sea, but over all there is the presence of the
Spirit; evil comes because duty is disregarded;
the gods are the shadows of men, many times
enlarged; but over all is the brooding and up-
lifting spirit, neither man nor the shadow of
man. And this religious poem, full of the

peculiar sanctity of literature, is a divine
masterpiece; it is of ideals, not of facts; it is
romantic; it is full of aspiration, in spite of
what the classicists may say. It is something
which M. Zola or Mr. Ibsen or Mr. Thomas
Hardy or any of the gentlemen with theories
of art might not blush to have written. It is
acknowledged by them to be greater than anything by M. Anatole France, or the late M.
Renan, or Maeterlink or even Mr. George
Meredith! Odysseus may be looked on as
realistic when he makes his final arrangements
with Penelope's suitors; but it is not a realism
after the manner of the heroes of the works of
the late M. de Maupassant;—Penelope remains
chaste. M. Zola or Mr. Ibsen or even the
ethical Flaubert would have abolished that
detail of idealism.

If all great odes outside the Bible were not
reflections of Pindar, I might put some of our
noble odes in English before his; for what other
language is so rich in great odes? From the
"Epithalamion" of Spenser to Lowell's "Commemoration," what a glittering throng! And
the elegies!—from "Lycidas" to Longfellow's
last song over his departing years! And, like
their great father, Pindar, how religious they
are; the sanctity and the dignity of literature
are theirs. Even the Thanatopsis is more
godly than careless critics have imagined and
Shelley's "Adonaïs" is more religious than the
man. And what is the meaning of that poem
loved of the poets, Keat's "Ode to a Grecian
Urn," but the inevitable longing for immor-

tality? And the cry of the exiled soul sounds all through the "Ode to the Nightingale." Only God Himself could keep the longing for Him out of poetry; and He has never done it.

A realistic poem would seem as amazing as a blue rose, which, let us hope, science may never try to produce. When Crabbe and Wordsworth are realistic, they cease to be poets. Rossetti tried to make a modern realistic poem; he called it "Jenny;" it deserved to be forgotten. To set a poet to the producing of a realistic work of literature would be like the asking of Raphael to leave his Madonnas to paint a picture of a dead crow.

Great literature expresses all life, but transmutes while expressing it; its halo surrounds even the coarser things. From the sweet and fine little pastorals of Theocritus to that great piece of literature, the Symposium of Plato, we find the Greek life and its ways sanctified by the ideal; and the expression of this ideal is instinct of immortality, which is religious. The amiable people who have a habit of classing literature with artificial flowers and album verses or with the Paul-and-Virginia kind of book probably do not as a rule put the "Symposium" under the head of "belles-lettres." The phrase "belles-lettres" is a delusion and a snare; it never meant anything, except in aristocratic salons. Whatever is beautiful and sweet and true, personally expressed, is literature. Who would call the poetry in St. Thomas "belles-lettres?" Dante only begun to fathom the depths of poetry in St. Thomas. And St. Paul, in English, is one of the strongest makers of literature that we have, however rough and ready his style may be in Greek. Take his definition of charity. There is beautiful truth beautifully and personally expressed. It is literature; it is more — it is poetry.

Vergil means to be religious; he is not so spontaneously religious as Homer, nor so spontaneous in any way as Theocritus. The Idyls of Theocritus are not wholly of the earth. The taint of paganism is upon them, but through the sweetest of them is the longing for something beyond the monotonous life of the shepherd. The reeds are not mere reeds by the river, for the breath of unseen creatures blows through them. The prize for the singing of Daphnis is a vase, but a vase valued because the things carved upon it are immortal. Theocritus does not sing of comfort, which is the object of modern materialist. His shepherds are content with the cyprus and the anemone, if they can but read the beauty beyond mere mortal knowing in the laurel, in the silver pool into which Hylas was dragged by the naiads — if they can but hear the notes of the waxed piper telling of vague splendors. To the shepherds the star appeared; for they, living among the marvels of nature, believing in things beyond nature, were ready to accept its coming with the docility of childlike faith.

It requires no extravagant stretch of imagination to interpret Vergil's meaning in the

fifth eclogue as an allusion to the coming of
the Saviour. And, if Seneca's tragedies are
turgid and dull, his dicta in other forms of
literature have induced the learned to believe
that he had been very near St. Paul. Literature at its best has always been full of aspiration. Poetry, its apex, has risen to the very
face of the sun itself. The sign of the great
poet is his reverence for woman—his religious
reverence for woman. It was reserved for the
purest and the best of all forms of religion to
offer the ideal woman to the worship of the
world. But woman, in all pre-Christian ages
reflected by poetry, held in one hand the gar-
ment hem of the known or unknown God,
while with the other she led men from the
dust. The moment the poet sings reverently
of womanhood, that moment he becomes
religious. The moment that he drags her and
himself to the mud beneath his feet, the light
of the rainbow of promise ceases to play about
him. Andromache and Helen are far apart,
and so are Penelope and Clytemnestra.
Woman, fallen, is in all literature, the worker
of evil; woman, faithful, is the helper and
consoler. The pagan ideal, expressed in
poetry, was only a vague prophecy of the
Christian ideal of womanhood; it was enough
to make the great old literature sacred. And,
later, not even Goethe, who was many-sided,
but almost untouched on any side by the beauty
of Christianity, could escape the religious ideal
of womanhood. In "Faust," it is the woman
who helps the man up to the feet of the Glorious

Mother. To go back to the mightiest of all poets, Dante, we find that he is, of all, the most Christian. And the ideal of womanhood glows above the Divine Comedy — Bella, his mother, Beatrice, Santa Lucia, the Mother of God, they lead the fearful soul from out the wood to the Beatific Vision itself.

The poet may not be true to his ideal in his daily life. Often, he keeps his worst; but when he enters into the exercise of his vocation, the gleam which is not of earth, which is as mystic as Arthur's Excalibur, shines upon him. Even Heinrich Heine, a satyr with a clouded soul, could not escape it; a poet may commit suicide in order to get beyond the reach of religion, but he only flees from hope and loses it. The unbeliever cries out, "My God! I do not believe in God;" and Julian, "Thou hast conquered, Galilean!" The poet, in spite of himself, must be religious. Similarly, the writer of prose, though he may belong to a school which tries to ignore Christ, runs everywhere against the fact of Christianity. The late Guy de Maupassant was a realist of the realists; life to him was a clinic and death the charnel-house. Yet the last words of his last printed work were a priest's plea for Christianity.

De Maupassant's priest, in "L'Angelus,"— the fragment found after his death among his papers — makes statements that would not stand the test of sound theology; they are "syllogismes de M. Prudhomme;" but, when we remember the materalism, the degraded philosophy of his works, we listen with amazement to these posthumous words of the man who yesterday was great in France.

"Qui sait?" says the Abbe Marvaux to the young invalid, who has blasphemed Providence. "Le Christ aussi a peut-être été trompé par Dieu dans sa mission, comme nous le sommes. Mais il est devenu Dieu lui même pour la terre pour, notre terre miserable, pour notre petite terre couverte de souffrants et de manants. Il est Dieu, notre Dieu, mon Dieu, et je l'aime de tout mon cœur d'homme et de toute mon âme de prêtre. O maître crucifié sur le Calvaire, je suis à toi, ton fils et ton serviteur." — "Mais le Christ, chez qui toute pitié, toute grandeur, toute philosophie, toute connaissance de l'humanité, sont descendues on ne sait d'où, qui fut plus malheureux que les plus misérables, qui naquit dans une étable et mourut cloué sur un tronc d'arbre, en nous laissant à tous la seule parole de vérité qui soit sage et consolante, pour vivre en ce triste endroit, celui-là, c'est mon Dieu, c'est mon Dieu, a moi." And even M. Zola was forced to describe a human being with a soul in "Le Rêve;" his hand showed some stiffness in the attempt — and perhaps it was a concession, not to the ideal, but to idealists in the Academy.

"Poets," writes a brilliant man in a late number of the *Edinburgh Review*, "are the prophets of each age. They express the highest thoughts of the generations in which they live and work. Judged by this test, at any rate,

Tennyson at once rises to the highest standard, since he was essentially an interpreter of the thoughts which were occupying the best and highest minds among us.''

Since literature has become democratic, the novel has crowded aside the poet—even a poet so much in accord with the best of his time as Tennyson.

It is to the modern novel we go for the tendencies of modern literature. The time looks on the novel as its epic, its chronicle. The reign of the drama is past, the satire has become the joke of the comic paper—as Gulliver's biting cynicism has become a book for boys who miss the bitterness in it. It may be that there are few poets who sing and that people like better to find their poetry in prose. The novel has even begun to preach, and that is a sign of decay. Not so very long ago a poem by Sir Walter Scott or Byron or Tennyson was almost an epoch; and somewhat later, a book by Swinburne or William Morris was an event. It is unfortunate that Byron is remembered by his sins, for surely there is enough in all his thousands of eloquent lines to show that he had at times the sanctity which ought to accompany the expression of beauty through the word. Sir Walter never lost sight of the kindly Light, and Tennyson always feels the influence of the Christ, Christ that Is, however far from Him he may look in his search for the Christ to be. Milton, before him, greater, more sonorous, less delicate, gave to woman—the pure and womanly woman—that

reverence in poetry which he denied to her in
real life.   He was transfigured when he wrote;
and it would be well if we could think of the
makers of literature only in their moments of
transfiguration.   Milton dared not be logical
by depicting the redemption of the wrong
wrought by his lovely Eve with the glowing
colors which Puritanism denied to Christ and
the Mother of Christ.   But, for all that, in
spite of the failure of "Paradise Regained,"
through his lack of sympathy with the instrument of the Incarnation, Milton is grandly
religious when he is noblest in the utterances
of his incomparable cadences.   The music of
each poet since Milton — the music of a great
organ, — every now and then soars through
the many tones of Wordsworth and Aubry De
Vere and Tennyson.   And this music is an
echo from the harmonies of Dante and the
melodies of Petrarch.   Milton, like all poets,
rose above his time, yet he was tainted, like
all poets, with the miasma of his time.   But
the principle of truth and the instinct of
beauty—that instinct, cultivated by the Italian
he loved—were strong within him.   Puritanism
could not destroy them, though he did not
escape its influence.   To miss the religion in
Milton, to close "Paradise Lost" because the
rebellion of his youth makes discord, is to
assume that a "sinless literature could come
of sinful man;"[1] to act as if poetry might
bring not only an angel but a God to earth to
make saints of all men.

[1] Newman: Idea of a University.

He who believes in democracy would be
foolish to hold that belief, if literature were
not a thing groping for God or fleeing with
the velocity of light to Him; for literature
reflects man. Through it man must be studied.
When literature fails us in the past, we are in
the mist. Archæology comes to our aid; but
the inscription on stone, the fragments of a
façade, or of an urn, are not so convincing or
satisfying as the written page presenting both
the idea and the impression, the great thought
and the mood of the moment. The Gothic
cathedral is the reflection of centuries when
literature spoke slightly, and yet it tells the
same tale as literature. It reflects man; his
hopes — above all, his *hopes* — his fears, his
temptations, the anxieties of his daily life.
There are strange domestic imps and elves in
the dark corners of its stalls, and from its
roof — as from the roof at Notre Dame of
Paris — hideous chimeras scowl and snarl.
The motions of the senses are not omitted; they
are depicted rude and naked. But the spires
point to God; all the details of the artist join
in a massive throng towards the tabernacle,
and the majestic arches, in their haste upward,
strike together and remained fixed forever.
Then literature, in its many forms, reflects
man; but man with his face turned to God,
even though the monstrous chimeras and the
brutal imps flit before him; even from literature as "degenerate" as that of François Villon
of the elder time, there comes the last cry of
poor De Maupassant, "C'est mon Dieu,—c'est
mon Dieu, a moi!"

Even Goethe, who felt that he was a Titan, admits that genius is bound by its limitations: "By his limitations is the master known." And the strongest of his bonds is the one that chains him to God.

If this were not so, if literature had not its sanctity, if there were not a tabernacle in the heart of the poet as in the heart of a church, if all the logical flutings and grandiose diapasons did not rush together on their way to God, how could we believe that the rule of the people is good! or that ultimate good can come from it! Literature is what man is; man is what literature is, and what the literature of his forefathers has helped to make him. Without literature how can man be known! or know himself! At a glowing line he feels the awakening of the slumbering ideal within him. The poet without has thrilled to life the poet within; and every man bears the poet within him. "Man," Newman says, "is a being of genius, passion, intellect, conscience, power. He exercises these various gifts in various ways, in great deeds, in great thoughts, in heroic acts, in hateful crimes. Literature records them all to the life." It aspires as man aspires; in this aspiration is the hope of the race. It may take the form of patriotism and seem to leave out God, but the love of country must find God or die. It may praise human love, but love must be tinged with the divine or it cloys.

Shakespere, who might have braved the utmost, dared not go beyond the "Beschränk-

ung" of Goethe. Religion is in the air of all
his great plays. One has only to compare
"Measure for Measure" with Goethe's "Elec-
tive Affinities," or Thomas Hardy's "Jude,"
or Balzac's "Père Goriot," to find how religious he was in comparison with the modern
"seer" who claims to draw a theory from life.
Cordelia, in "King Lear," should be a pagan;
she is a Christian of the Christians. The gods
of the King, her father, are not the pagan
gods—not the fates of Œdipus—for they admit
the free will of their subjects. It is not fate,
but Lear that has wrought the ruin. Claudius
sins deliberately; his conscience is open-eyed,
his judgment of right and wrong is not per-
plexed. Romeo and Juliet try to mount to
the sun on the waxen wings of passion; they
fall, crushed. It is not fate that crushes
them; the sanctity of the marriage tie is not
reproached, nor is Christian morality jeered
at. In "Macbeth," who can escape the idea
of God? In "Othello" Iago is a man who has
chosen evil. Like the condemned one in
Dante's "Inferno," whose soul is in torture
while his body is possessed of the devil on
earth, is Iago. The horrible evil of Iago
makes one turn to the good. Desdemona dies.
Malice and jealousy have destroyed a creature
compact of light: who is not more in love with
the virtues that might have preserved her?
Leontes, in "A Winter's Tale," is coarse,
sensual; the grossness of his thoughts have
made him so; he believes in no woman. The
woman, too pure for his belief, teaches him

another lesson through suffering; and who can dispute the religion of this teaching? The purest of religions is founded on the purity of the Woman; and the poet who upholds the purity of her sex does the work of religion. In "As You Like It" Jaques, the pessimist, interferes for the sanctity of marriage when Touchstone would imitate his Tudor betters and make devorce easy; and the joyous and spring-like love of Orlando and Rosalind is an honest love—a love that, with the blessing of the Church, will become sacramental. About the foot of the work of the poet there may be lizards and the coarser weeds, but on its top the eagles face the sun. "If you would in fact have a literature of saints," Newman says, "first of all have a nation of them."

In every age literature has been held more sacred by its professors than it is held to-day. The modern oracle speaks not for beings who bend the knee before the tripod, but for those that drop coin of the realm into the "slot" of the machine it has adopted. The makers of literature are only the "filles de joie," Robert Louis Stevenson once said; and no maker of literature ever uttered a more debased sentiment. When literature puts on the garb of the dancer and lives for "joie" and money, one of the glories of life will have departed. But no people can live without ideals, and literature will always uphold, reflect, and illuminate these ideals. This it has always done; and, in spite of the devotees of mere form at the end of our century, it has done so

among the greatest of this century. Tennyson and Newman, Aubrey de Vere and Ruskin,
Longfellow and Lowell; there is no lack of
beauty or dignity or sanctity in the works of
these men.

Tennyson is as reverent as Newman; but he
"feels" that God must exist; he has not the
logic or the faith of the chaunter of the "Dream
of Gerontius." With Newman, life is the life
of the soul and mind; the Inspired Word and
Cicero are his guides. He is a humanist; he
writes for the elect; but, as he himself says,
"the elect are few to choose out of, and the
world is inexhaustible."

Tennyson is of the world, but he idealizes
and lights up the world. Theocritus, Byron,
Spenser, Keats — above all, Milton — and
Chaucer influence him; he takes his own
whenever he finds it, and makes bits out of
Dante as musical as they are in Tuscan. He
is pure and true; in his best work he turns to
the highest manifestations of religion. He
strikes the harp of time and sings of St.
Agnes and Sir Galahad, and of the Lady of
Shallott, who loved from her serene place the
forms of earth for a moment. He sings an
allegory. He cannot rid himself of the mysticism of Sir Galahad and Sir Persival and the
thought of the Holy Grail. He might have
tuned his lyre to lower themes, but genius
chooses to limit itself. The old stories of Sir
Thomas Malory held him and the light flashing
from the sword Excalibur led him on. And
the three queens were with him. And the

symbolic azure, vert and red fell upon him
through the stained glass in the religious light
he loved; and so he wrote "The Idyls of the
King." There arose women and men of the
present in the garb of the past — men and
women somewhat archaic, as the figures
composed for tapestry by Sir Edward Burne
Jones; but men and women, with the God of
the Christians in their minds, if not always in
their hearts. Some think the form of Tennyson's poem to be too exquisite; but there is
vitality beneath it. The poet who could, in
an age in which most men call perplexity
doubt, express the chastity of Arthur and
the repentance of Guinevere could have had
no timid question as to the sacredness of
his office. Tennyson drew one generation towards purity as Newman led it towards faith;
and one helps the other.

Wordsworth took himself as a priest from
the beginning, a very Melchisedec of poetry.
His chasuble was the color of the sun when it
is low, and his stole was of the tints of the
rainbow. No great poet, except Dante, ever
felt more deeply the sanctity of his office.
Aubrey de Vere has not yet been heard of by
all the people; he is of the elect, but the time
is coming when he, after waiting, like Wordsworth, shall be heard "urbi et orbi." In the
epilogue to "Asolando," Robert Browning
cries:

"Never doubted clouds would break,
Never dreamed, though right were worsted, wrong would
        triumph,
Held we fall to rise, are baffled to fight better, sleep to
        wake."

And earlier, he says:

> "What is it that I hunger but for God?
> My God, my God, let me for once look on Thee
> As though nought else existed, we alone!"

His soul cried out; being a poet, he could not escape God.

Longfellow, the son of the Puritans, chooses for his master-work the union of faith and purity—the Christian ideal of the woman—in "Evangeline;" and Whittier, the Quaker, turns to the saints of Rome for subjects as his life-tide ebbs away. William Morris, "the idle singer of an empty day," looks to the times of faith for his heroes and his greatness shows. Even Voltaire, when he touched poetry seriously, tried to be religious, and he even dedicated his tragedy, "Mahommed," to the Pope.

No better example of the amazing influence of poetry than this can be cited!

The poet in the olden days was priestly; his songs were as revelations from above to the children of nature. He did not escape God, no matter how unworthy to utter His name he might be. If there were no priests the sacerdotal element would rest, not only in the consciences, but in the literature of the people. And yet, with its sanctity, the best literature has its corruptions. It has its Dante; but Dante also has his bitterness and Shakespere his coarseness, and Cervantes likewise his. True, but listen to what Newman says to those who would close the gates of the temple because all the things of life are carved in its stalls — imps and chimeras that might shock and

offend and perhaps teach. Newman speaks
of one shut out because the clay feet of the
god are seen and the nimbus forgotten. "You
have refused him the masters of human
thought, who would in some sense have
educated him, because of their incidental cor-
ruption. You have shut up from him those
whose thoughts strike home to our hearts,
whose words are proverbs, whose names are
indigenous to all the world, who are the
standard of their mother tongue, and the pride
and boast of their countrymen—Homer, Aristotle, Cervantes, Shakespere—because the old
Adam smelt rank in them; and for what have
you reserved him. You have given him 'a
liberty unto' the multitudinous blasphemy of
his day. You have made him free of its newspapers, its reviews, its magazines, its novels,
its controversial pamphlets, of its parliamen-
tary debates, its law proceedings, its platform
speeches, its songs, its drama, its theatre, of
its enveloping, stifling atmosphere of death.
You have succeeded but in this — in making
the world his university."

The roots of the lotus are in the slime, yet,—
the myths of India declare,—the serene Buddha
sits in the golden heart of the flower. The
life of the poet, like the life of all men, is fed
from below, but it flames upward; and even
through the gloom of Pantheism it struggled
towards the Throne. At last from the soul of
Dante it touched the very feet of Christ.

IV. SOME ASPECTS OF AN AMERICAN ESSAYIST.

THOSE results of meditation, to which the French give the name "Pensées," are not common in English literature. The mention of them at once recalls Pascal and Vauvenargues—to whom Voltaire was so much indebted — de la Rochefoucauld, the Abbé Roux and a half dozen professed writers of the more or less epigrammatic "Thought" or "Reflection." George Meredith has tried to make the epigram an integral part of style, with much the same effect as Carlyle's attempt to be unusual. But outside of Emerson and Bishop Spalding no great writer in America occurs to the mind as a maker of aphorisms; and when it is a question of the form which the latter has adopted for his principal prose works, we find it described as "epigrammatic," "aphoristic," or "axiomatic." It is true that it partakes of all three, — to which may be added the qualities which make prose poetic,— warmth of imagination and music of rhythm. But, in the consideration of Bishop Spalding's prose, which has caused many amazing comparisons, the key of the enigma is lost unless we remember that the prose of his essays is the prose of an orator. Essentially, it resembles the prose of no modern, except Emerson. And the cause of this resemblance lies in the fact that the methods of construction employed by both Emerson and Spalding are no doubt similar. And the prose of Emerson and the prose of Spalding appear to have been written to be spoken. When Pascal says: "Les inventions des hommes vont en avançant de siècle en siècle. La bonté et la malice du monde en général est de même," and then breaks off to assert that "La force est la reine du monde, et non pas l'opinion; l'opinion est celle qui use de la force,"[1] we know that these aphorisms were made to be read. When Spalding says: "If thou take more pleasure in seeing thy prejudices overcome by truth than in finding arguments to confirm thee in them, thy studies shall cheer thee and lead thee to fairer words," and adds: "Cremonini, hearing that Galileo had discovered the moons of Jupiter, refused to turn his telescope to the planet, lest he should find that Aristotle had been wrong," we are sure that these words are to be uttered aloud.

When DeQuincy and Ruskin make their long periods, we are aware at once that they are intended for the closet; and no student can get at the secret of Bishop Spalding's style without serious attention to the manner in which he uses his tools to attain his object. In truth, no criticism of literary form is valid unless the critic can get at the artistic intention of the writer; and the most essential canon of the artist is that he may not utter at random.

---

[1] Pensées de Pascal, p. 209: Paris: Garnier.

but must be completely master of the power
of his phrase. Whether conscious or unconscious, Bishop Spalding is, in this respect,
a thorough artist. Style, he says somewhere,
is the thought itself forcing its way to the
light; but no style could be, more thoroughly
than his own, against the theory that the mute
Milton must speak sooner or later; for it is
the result of careful practice, directed according to the surest canons of literary expression.
He has solved the problems which have vexed
many artists in letters, — how to denude the
oration of those tricks which make it possible
only when spoken,—how to make the spoken
word impress the reader as it impressed the
hearer. This problem Lowell solved in his
famous "Democracy," and Spalding has done
it, too, even more effectually, in his four
books, "Education and the Higher Life,"
"Things of the Mind," "Means and Ends of
Education," and "Thoughts and Theories of
Life and Education."

In the first of these volumes, in the article
on "Self-Culture,"[1] he says: "As the painter
takes pallet and brush, the musician his instrument, each to perfect himself in his art, so
he who desires to learn how to think should
take the pen, and day by day write something
of the truth, the hope and faith, which make
him a living man." Here we have the theory
on which Bishop Spalding has found his
unique style; it is a protest against "art for

---

[1] A. C. McClurg & Co., Chicago.

art's sake," but it does not ignore art; it makes it necessary. If, with him the style is the man, as well as the word, it has become so only after that stern apprenticeship, that incessant and sometimes despairing practice which enters into the life of every artist. "And it will frequently happen," he had already said, "that there will be permanent value in what is written, not to please the crowd or to flatter a capricious public opinion, or to win gold or applause, but simply in the presence of God and one's soul to bear witness to truth."

The artist in letters badly needs this message, since the clamor of the time for new things draws him, in spite of his better self, into the glare and the struggle of a social condition which his brother of a statelier time, when letters were aristocratic, did not know. The public demands, and the author answers until his voice, once so rich and full, grown so in the great silence which produces the best, becomes a thin falsetto. He must sing over and over again, with no time for growth, and with variations, the song that the people like.

The methods of Bishop Spalding, as one easily discovers through internal evidence, are practical protests against inartistict work; it is not difficult to trace the processes by which his style has been formed or the means by which his thoughts have been developed. Sincerity, the absence of selfishness, in the sense which makes that word mean the contemplation of self, and simplicity of utterance,

are marked characteristics of his intention and
manner. The great difficulty in the way of
the student of the technique of his work has
been that of comparison with other writers.
Every author of importance has his literary
pedigree; he has also a system for the development of his technique quite as stringent as
that of the athlete. We can trace the philosophy of Bishop Spalding and be astonished at
the wonderful power of synthesis, by which
the systems merge into logical sequence, and
at the unerring knowledge by which he detects
the evil in them while retaining the good; the
student, however, who can easily find the
literary genealogy of Newman and Tennyson,
Emerson, Mallock and Lilly, begins at once
to make the conclusion that Bishop Spalding is
a literary descendant of Emerson. There is
a superficial resemblance; both feed deeply
on Plato and Montaigne; both write the
conclusions of thinking, and both leave the
means by which these conclusions are reached
to the imagination of the reader. It is plain
that both have adopted the legend "no day
without a line," and that they accumulate
a vast amount of material in this way; but
here the resemblance ends. Emerson has no
firmer basis for his ethical demands than
Spencer; he loves or fears no gods, and the
meaning of his great predecessors thus escapes
him. St. Augustin and St. Thomas are not
of his ancestors, nor is Dante; but he means
that Marcus Aurelius and Epictetus shall be.
Emerson sees all things through a frosty

mist; he shows us a dim rainbow, but points
out no bridge between us and that arch of
light; the past does not exist for him, because
he lacked the imagination and feeung necessary to the realization of it.　He is of the
present,—of the New World entirely, getting,
through his own personality, meanings out of
the great masters which were not always in
them.　In this way he made them his own;
few writers are more literary and few less
philosophical than Emerson.

Emerson saw the rainbow of the ideal and
assumed the attitude of its priest and worship-
per, but the fire in his temple was of green
wood, so that between the smoke and the
frosty mist the beauty of his object is obscured.
Nevertheless we Americans owe much to him,
for he was no materialist, and so long as he is
read, our country cannot become "a sort of
Chinese Empire, with three hundred millions
of human beings, and not a divine man or
woman."　Indeed, the debt that this United
States of America owe to Emerson must always
be very great; and if he is not potent at present,
it is because our world is going further from
his ideals of living, and because he offers no
solid, religious basis for his ethical demands.

Bishop Spalding, on the other hand, is
compact of imagination and feeling.　Not
only has he the glow of vital and passionate
conviction, but the premises of his conclusions
are so firm that he does not need to express
them.　It is not necessary that he should
prove the existence of Christ, God and Man,

or the spotlessness of the Mother of God. It does not go with his temperament or with the temperament of his people that he shall utter terms of endearment every time he alludes to the Redeemer or the Co-Redemptrix. Every page he writes is fulgent with the glow from faith. It is with the result of Christianity, — with the appreciation of the teachings of the Catholic Church that he concerns himself. In him, faith fuses the heart and the mind. In "Ideals," he says: "Whatever may be said in praise of culture, of its power to make its possessor at home in the world of the best thought, the purest sentiment, the highest achievements of the race; of the freedom, the mildness, the reasonableness of the temper it begets; of its aim at completeness and perfection, it is nevertheless true, that if it be sought apart from faith in God and devotion to man, its tendency is to produce an artificial and unsympathetic character. The primal impulse of our nature is to action; and unless we can make our thought a kind of deed, it seems to be vain and unreal; and unless the harmonious development of all the endowments which make the beauty and dignity of human life, give us new strength and will to work with God for the good of men, sadness and a sense of failure fall upon us. To have a cultivated mind, to be able to see things on many sides, to have wide sympathy and power of generous appreciation,—is most desirable, and, without something of all this, not only is our life narrow and uninteresting, but our energy is turned in wrong directions, and our very religion is in danger of losing its catholicity." He admits with St. Paul that "knowledge puffeth up," but he also makes the distinction which prevents the indolent from quoting the apostle of the Gentiles in defense of ignorance.

Emerson is too often, like Pascal, merely a writer of aphorisms, unconnected, expressed without even unseen logical links. This is never so apparent as when we compare Spalding with him. Emerson is often a conscious maker of phrases, and he would be an epigrammist, did he ever aim to be witty. Pascal and Vauvenargues and La Rochefoucauld and the Abbé Roux write "Pensées" as a man writes a sonnet, with intense regard for the form; Emerson has this regard for form, too—but it is merely that the form should be oracular; therefore nearly all his essays are made up of deliverances of the moment without regard to the binding thread of syllogism that should underlie all convincing work. His thoughts are brilliants, imbedded in enamel, never touching one another. In Bishop Spalding's essays,—the essays of an orator,—the syllogistic thread is always there.[1]

The young and the eager, the old and the weary, demand two opposite forms of expression. And the expression of both Emerson and Spalding appeals more to the young than to the old; — because the imagination is vivid in the young. But the tendency of the art of

[1] Education and the Higher Life, p. 21.

printing is to induce us to demand that our thinking shall be done for us in sight. Emerson does not answer to this, because he reflects light on a certain thought of Plato or Montaigne's,—and his task is done with the flash. Spalding's thoughts are chained to the central thesis. Like the links of an anchor, stretched from a wharf to a boat, they may be hidden under myriad sparkles, but they are solid and strong. Like all poets, whether they write in prose or verse, Bishop Spalding is a philosopher; but is he less an artist? One can best explain the apparent defect of his Emersonian abruptness and lack of sequence by drawing an illustration from the art of painting in the words of Vernon Lee.[1] We see in time, she says, as much as in space, so that much must be left to the imagination. "Titian, for instance, painted a background to the 'Sacred and Profane Love' whose light is considerably later on in the afternoon than the light in the figures of the foreground; and Lotto puts a moon and moonlit landscape behind his wicked turbaned lady with the stone-pinks, (his masterpiece at Bergamo) while illuminating his face with the last daylight. The color of the two halves of the picture seems rather to turn our soul to a chord, as it were of harmonious feeling, a chord of rapidly succeeding notes like the great ground-out chords of an organ, instead of pitching it to a meagre unison. For pictures

---

[1] "Imagination in Modern Art." *The Fortnightly Re riew*, October, 1897.

like these are painted to please our soul by means of the eye, not to convince our eye idly, with no profit to our soul."

Bishop Spalding paints his pictures for the soul; but he does not paint them for the inert soul. He has disdain for those who read only as they run. "A woman," he says, "cannot hope to make a sage or a saint or a hero of the man who loves her, but she may of the child." The sentence ends here; he takes up the thread of the thought with "Contempt of women is the mark of a crude mind or of a corrupt heart." There is the link, — or many links, according to the activity of one's own mind— between his sentences. He returns to the child and to the influence of the mother: "What strength is there not in the rich joyfulness of youth, bursting forth into glad song and laughter, and passing lightly away from hardship and disappointment, out again to where the glorious sunshine plays upon the rippling waters and happy flowers. The very memory of it all comes back to us like a message from God to bid us be stout of heart and keep growing. Those we love sanctify for us the places where they have lived; the spots even where they have passed are sacred."[1]

Through each essay in these four volumes we can trace, beneath the abundance of aphorisms and the wealth of illustration, the thesis. And this makes one of the important differences that distinguish the two great American

---

[1] "Things of the Mind:" Views of Education, p. 22.

writers who raise their voices for plain living
and high thinking. The thesis in each essay
is boldly and directly stated; it appears and
reappears; it shines and glows; it is darkened
for a time, only to glance out of the shadows;
it is a running brook hidden at times beneath
foliage till it gathers into a cascade, but it is
always the same stream. Bishop Spalding
uses the privilege of the orator and reiterates
under every possible form the truths he is
forced to utter. In the first chapter of his[1]
latest book, he announces the central thought,
which he does not lose sight of. "In the
course of ages there have been a few in whose
company it is possible to think high thoughts
in a noble spirit; but there has been and is
but one with whom it is possible to lead the
life of the soul and feel that it is like the life
of God, — he is the Master Jesus Christ, who
alone makes us understand and realize that
God is our Father, and that our business on
earth is to grow into the divine image by right
living and doing.[2] The deeper and purer
one's religion, the higher and richer his moral
life; and as moral worth increases, faith in
God is confirmed." The "Leitmotif" comes
again and again; he plays it softly, — then he
brings it out thunderously, fugue on fugue.
"Though thou thyself fail, rejoice that it has
been given to another to do nobly; for if thou
art capable of envy, thou art incapable of

---

[1] Thoughts and Theories of Life and Education. Chicago,
1897.

[2] Ibid, p. 18.

wisdom. Since truth is the highest, being the center of goodness and love, truthfulness is the best. If God has made thee capable of doing any real thing, thou must do it, or in all eternity it will not be done. The highest is for thee, since God wills to give Himself to thee.''

In the light of faith, who can go to Carlyle for sympathy or consolation? With the great Scotch colorist, "God wills to give Himself to thee'' would be a mere phrase. The traces, not only of German scholarship, but of Germanic construction, are visible in all Spalding's prose work. The influences of Goethe and the best of Kant are evident in many places. Bishop Spalding recognizes the sanctity that each had not lost and could not lose. The effect of the Germanic word-study is to dissipate the Latin haze which hangs about the sentences of too many ecclesiastics who achieve their instruction only through the old Roman tongue. Though the cadence of the paragraph is sometimes Germanic, the phrase is never affected, and ease of apprehension is greatly helped by the direct Englishing of thoughts which would have been obscure if Latinized. Occasionally one wonders why Bishop Spalding does not take advantage of the German cadence to slip in a compound word or two, and thus become a pioneer in the restoration of valuable forms which the Anglo-Saxon, in its process of change, has almost irretrievably lost.

The longing for simplicity that permeates

Wordsworth runs through these essays. Some passages remind us of Wordsworth's sonnet against the substitution of pictures for plain type in periodicals, —

> "Avaunt this vile abuse of pictured page,
> Must eyes be all in all, the tongue and ear
> Nothing? Heaven keep us from a lower stage."[1]

Bishop Spalding's plea for the simple life has not the passionate insistance of Wordsworth; it seems, in truth, to have somewhat of the aristocratically intellectual tone of Horace; but study will show us that the recurrence is due not to the mere personal intellectual disdain for the vulgar, but to the serious belief that the best props of patriotism are elevation of the mind and frugal living. Bishop Spalding does not seem to consider doubt or the paralysis that comes of doubt; he sees plainly that few men really doubt the eternal verities. He holds that materialism, the pride of life, the lust of power,—what are called by the Philistine "facts of life," are the real dangers to human happiness. He does not shriek against the Philistine, like Heine and Matthew Arnold; he is too serious for that. He faces popular fallacies with calmness, but with penetrating eyes that hold no pity for lies or shams. The idols held up by the newspapers are scorned by him; wealth is good as an instrument for the higher development of the man; he hears that Americans love education for all as the

---

[1] Illustrated Books and Papers: Poems of Wm. Wordsworth; p. 184.

core of their hearts, and he disperses a mock nimbus with "When we Americans shall have learned to believe with all our hearts and with all the strength of irresistible conviction that a true educator is a more important, in every way a more useful, sort of man than a great railway king, or pork butcher, or captain of industry, or grain buyer, or stock manipulator, we shall have begun to make ourselves capable of perceiving the real scope of public school education."[1]

What wise American believes that legislation will cure the present evils of society? What observant man regards the increase of wealth and the inordinate desire for it as guarantees of the stability of the state? Or seriously holds that the organization of many will solve problems which, Christianity teaches us, can only be answered by the heart of each man? Bishop Spalding sees that the remedy which many of our legislators, our educators, and even our preachers, pretend not to see lies in the application of a higher standard to the realities of personal life. Where every boy is expected to grow rich or fail to reach the average American ideal, such teaching as that of Bishop Spalding will not be heard eagerly or received with plaudits. The strength of the early Americans lay in the disregard of the little wants for the greater needs. "Wordsworth was praised to me in Westmoreland," writes Emerson in his essay on "Culture,"

---

[1] Scope of Public School Education p. 150.   •

"for having afforded to his country neighbors
an example of a modest household where comfort and culture were secured without display.
And a tender boy who wears his rusty cap and
outgrown coat, that he may secure the coveted
place in college and the right in the library, is
educated to some purpose. There is a great
stock of selfdenial and manliness in poor and
middle-class houses, in town and country, that
has not got into literature and never will, but
that keeps the earth sweet; that saves in super-
fluities and spends on essentials; that goes
rusty and educates the boy; that sells the
horse, but builds the school; works early and
late, takes two looms in the factory, three
looms, six looms, but pays off the mortgage
on the paternal farm, and then goes back
cheerfully to work again."

There has been much heard of late about
farm mortgages, but anything like this method
of paying them off has not been seriously considered. In the stories of rural life in America,
which are supposed to represent things in a
better state—the Kansas or Missouri mortgage
is generally paid off by good luck in a horse
race or a fortunate stroke in speculation.
Bishop Spalding echoes the Spartan cry from
the experience of every nation that has lived.
It was the lesson that Joseph, the foster-father
of our Lord taught, as he worked in wood.
[1] "Wealth and numbers we have," the Bishop

---

[1] Things of the Mind : Patriotism, p. 230.

writes, "and all the strength which material civilization can give. What we lack is a new man to represent fitly this new world. Great things must be enhanced by great characters, or matter will prevail over spirit, and the soul become inferior to its setting. The special vice of the American is the breathless haste with which he works for success, which he generally takes to mean money. Whatever is restful, as reflection and meditation, gives him qualms of conscience; he is ashamed to be at leisure. He thinks, watch in hand, as he eats, with his eye on the daily market report. He seems always afraid lest he forget or neglect something, and so miss an opportunity to make a dollar. This workingman's haste, this alertness for a chance to turn a penny, is fatal to distinction of thought and behavior; it destroys the sense for form, proportion, and grace. Hence, this type of American in all the relations of life is quick, sharp and abrupt. In his intercourse with friends and relations, with women and children, he is preoccupied by thoughts of business, and seems to say: 'Appreciate my politeness, for time is money.' His natural inclination is to marry a wife with as little ceremony as he buys a horse. Joyful occasions are almost as unwelcome to him as the sad, for both alike are interruptions of business. If he is poor, he works with the hope of becoming rich; if he is rich, he works from dread of poverty. He can not take recreation without apology, as though he should say, 'I beg par-

don, but my health or my wife's health requires
this of me.' He writes a letter in the style of
a telegram, and would prefer to talk only
through a telephone from fear of being button-
holed. He looks forward to the time when he
shall travel a hundred instead of fifty miles an
hour, and in his rapid journeys he is all the
while thinking or talking of business or politics, which for him is mainly a question of
finance. The men in whom he takes interest
are money men and politicians. . . . A book, a
preacher, a play, like a mine or a railway, are
worth what they will sell for in the market.
What is dear is fine, and he will even submit
to all sorts of discomfort, if it is expensive. . . .
We lack self-control, and are borne forward
by this material movement, as the crest is
carried by the wave. We have lost relish for
a life which is simple, pure. moderate and
healthful.''

These are words of truth, fitly spoken. "If
we love our country,'' the essayist goes on to
say, "let us not be afraid to speak even unpleasant truth in this age when it has grown
to be the fashion to lie to the people, as
formerly men lied to kings.''

Bishop Spalding has been accused of lean-
ing towards the modern German philosophers—
Kant and Hegel—by critics who frighten children with these names, just as the Saracen
mothers horrified their offspring by threaten-
ing them with the devilish English led by the
Lion-Hearted. He plucks the good from these
men and he recognizes their genius, as one

may recognize the genius of Heine without approving of his changing opinions; his Catholicity and catholicity give him a power over American minds which few of us possess.[1] "A man of learning without philosophy," he says, "is, according to Kant, but a mathematical, historical, philological, geographical, or astronomical Cyclops. He lacks an eye."

According to Bishop Spalding, the one quality needed for the truest patriotism is that the citizen should be a man.[2] "To imagine, then, that we educate when we do nothing but sharpen the intellect is a shallow conceit. Wiser than the knowing are they who feel God's presence and man's sacredness, and who walk in lowliness of spirit. Dost thou think it desirable to be born rich or to attain political or commercial distinction and influence? Canst thou not see that they who are born rich, or who attain political or commercial distinction, rarely become true men, but lack the best insight and the highest virtue! Be thankful, then, for what in thy youth thou didst hold to be disadvantages and obstacles; for to them thou owest thy vocation to the pursuit of knowledge and the striving for excellence."

This is not palatable counsel; it is not the basis of popular education; youth in America is not taught to believe it; but what higher lesson can youth learn?

He who can hold, after reading Bishop

---

[1] Thoughts and Theories of Life and Education, p. 160.
[2] Ibid. p. 59.

Spalding, that the influence of the Church in
this country is for repression of the best in
man or for the development of the worst in
society and politics, must not be a Cyclops,
but utterly blind. Sufficient has been said
to sketch one or two aspects of the most
serious and many-sided of our American essay-
ists, — of whom one may say, as Principal
Shairp said of Newman,[1] that "his power
shows itself chiefly in the new and unlooked-
for way in which he touches into life old
truths, moral or spiritual, which all Christians
acknowledge, but most have ceased to feel."

---

[1] Principal Shairp's "Studies of Poetry," quoted in Newman's "My Campaign in Ireland."

THE ODE STRUCTURE OF COVENTRY PATMORE.

THE "Odes" of Coventry Patmore are so well known to students of metres and to the lovers of what is called the mystic quality in poetry, that they may be considered in the interest of both with unfailing profit. They owe much of their essence to St. Teresa and to St. John, and all that attracts the lovers of the science of poetic form in them is due to the force of this essence exerted to find adequate expression. It may be said that the practice adopted by Mr. Patmore is, like the later musical forms of Wagner, not a sign of regular progress, but a vagary, or a mere diversion from the regular track of progress. For instance, what apparently answers in music to verbal rhyme is easily discovered in the scores of Haydn and Mozart; the absence of this is noticeable in Beethoven and Wagner. In verse the continual rhyme, accompanied by the regular cæsura, is a distinguishing characteristic of Pope and Scott;—Patmore accepts the rhyme and the cæsura, but, in his noblest poems, uses them irregularly, or rather spontaneously by making the pause depend on feeling and the rhyme on the emphasis of accent. The practice of Patmore is a sign of a finer conception of the clothing of poetry. Whether the

(82)

changes in the musical forms be more than a vagary, I am not enough of a musician to know; but as to metres, I believe that Patmore's variations from classical English verse form indicate that the poetry of the twentieth century will achieve the expression of subtler meanings than the poetry of any preceding era. The change in Patmore's methods is evident only in the poems which to the refined sense of the world are beginning to be "great."

In these poems he feels rather than knows that finish and tone melody and harmony may be best reached by minimizing rhyme, which is often used "to cover a multitude of sins of harmony." In writing unrhymed verse, "the poet has to depend upon the melodious movement of the individual verses, pause-melody, and the general harmony of toning." Students, theoretical and practical, of the science and art of verse know that it requires all the forces of a poet to sustain himself without rhyme, — "which to the unskillful is often a veritable life-preserver, and the only power which keeps much unpoetical stuff afloat."[1]

There is a prejudice against the "domestic" poetry of Coventry Patmore in that class of minds which cannot tolerate even Wordsworth when he aims for simplicity and achieves simpleness. And yet there are many who love "The Angel in the House," and who find no fault with the jingling rhymes of "The Rosy Bosom'd Hours," — the story of a wedding journey:

---

[1] Dr. Corson: Primer of English Verse. Ginn & Co.

"At Dawlish, 'mid the pools of brine,
　　You stept from rock to rock,
One hand quick tightening upon mine,
　　One holding up your frock.

"On starfish and on weeds alone
　　You seemed intent to be,
Flashed those great gleams of hope unknown
　　From you, or from the sea?

"Ne'er came before, ah, when again
　　Shall come two days like these,
Such quick delight within the brain,
　　Within the heart such peace?

"I thought, indeed, by magic chance,
　　A third from heaven to win,
But as, at dusk, we reached Penzance,
　　A drizzling rain set in."

There are some, too, not appalled by the
close of "The Girl of All Periods":

"And Ben began to talk with her, the rather
Because he found out that he knew her father,
Sir Francis Applegarth, of Fenny Compton,
And danced once with her sister, Maud, at Brompton ;
And then he stared until he quite confused her,
More pleased with her than I, who but excused her ;
And, when she got out, he, with sheepish glances,
Said he'd stop, too, and call on old Sir Francis."

In justice, however, to the admirers of this
sort of poetry, let us quote Mr. Aubrey de
Vere:

"Of the longer poems which attempt exclu-
sively to describe the finer emotions of modern
society, the most original and most artistic is

Mr. Coventry Patmore's 'Angel in the House;' a poem," he adds, "which is better than a thousand *a priori* arguments in favor of the school to which it belongs. Others, instead of representing have caricatured modern life. They seem to have forgotten that the railway whistle and the smoke of the factory chimney are but accidents of our age, as powder and patch were accidents of the preceding one, and that the true life of the nineteenth century must lie deeper."[1]

In spite of Aubrey de Vere, one of the most acute and just of critics, it is difficult to enjoy a poem of realism without an ever-present fear that the tea-cups may fall or the piles of bread and butter come down suddenly. Tennyson's realism is so enameled that there seems to be less danger of breaking its surface; he gives it a pastoral character as artificially simple as an idyll of Theocritus and as elegant as a scene done by Watteau. The late Lord Lytton in "Lucile" escaped simpleness by becoming romantic. This, Patmore does not attempt; he goes on, with his recurrent rhymes, chronicling, with an audacity that is dazzling, the every-day affairs of life in a place where nothing ever happens. Miss Austen, in her most domestic novels, was not more realistic, and Crabbe's verses are tumultuous compared with his; but here, while confessing myself as of those who have prejudices, — not perhaps founded on principles, — against "The Angel

---

[1] Essays, Literary and Ethical. By Aubrey de Vere, LL. D. Macmillan & Co.

in the House," let me quote Aubrey de Vere again when he speaks of certain poets,—"With some the fancy acquires a daintiness which loses the fine in the superfine, and can only condescend to touch the honest realities of nature through the intercession of a white kid glove. Hence love is treated as if we live in a moonlight world, and were too delicate to bear sunshine. The converse evil has yet more debased the literature of many periods, especially in that diseased school which under the guise of celebrating passion, sings in reality the blind triumph of animal instincts thinly veiled. From these blemishes Mr. Patmore's work is entirely free."

These verses of domestic life may be delightful poems of the highest value; they are popular, and a thousand times above Mr. Tupper's "Proverbial Philosophy," which was also popular,—more popular indeed than anything written by Mr. Patmore. It would be absurd to make popularity the test of merit. And as to the structure, of these verses, which produces as monotonous an effect as the perpetual couplet rhymes of Pope, Mr. Patmore might offer in extenuation his "Night and Sleep," one of the most exquisitely musical poems in our language:

> "How strange at night to wake,
>   And watch while others sleep,
> 'Till sight and hearing ache
>   For objects that may keep
> The awful inner sense
>   Unroused, lest it should mark
> The life that haunts the emptiness
>   The horror of the dark!

> How strange at night the bay
>   Of dogs, how wild the note
> Of cocks that scream for day,
>   In homesteads far remote;
> How strange and wild to hear
>   The old and crumbling tower,
> Amid the darkness, suddenly
>   Take tongue and speak the hour !"

Although the music of "Night and Sleep" is not dependent upon the rhyme, it is plain,—as the form of poetry appeals to the ear,—that the rhyme is a gain; and yet one does not miss it in the fifth and seventh line of each stanza. The real musical charm of the poem, — only two stanzas, of four, are given here, — lies in the management of the rhythm. "We have only to *fill up* the measure in every line as well as in the seventh, in order to change this verse from the slowest and most mournful to the most rapid and most high-spirited of all English, the common eight-syllable quatrain," says Mr. Patmore in his "Essay on English Metrical Law," "a measure particularly recommended by the early critics, and continually chosen by poets in all times for erotic poetry on account of its joyful air. The reason of this unusual rapidity of movement is the unusual character of the eight-syllable verse as acatalectic, almost all other kinds of verse being catalectic on at least one syllable, implying a final pause of corresponding duration."

Mr. Patmore here shows that the rhyme in this lovely "Night and Sleep" is merely accessory, a lightly played accompaniment to a song that would be as beautiful a song without it, yet gaining a certain accent through this accompaniment, and that the real questions in all verse are of rhythm and of time.　Tennyson, whose technique, even in the use of sibilants, will bear the closest scrutiny, often proves the merely accessory value of rhyme, but in no instance more fully than in—

> " Tears, idle tears, I know not what they mean
> Tears from the depth of some divine despair
> Rise in the heart and gather in the eyes,
> In looking on the happy autumn fields,
> And thinking of the days that are no more."[1]

This is an exquisite lyric.　Until science analyzes more deeply the finest links that form the most elusive chains of harmony, and inspiration seizes the result of this analysis, there can be no more exquisite lyric.　It sings itself; rhyme would be superfluous, and no musical setting by a composer has hitherto succeeded in anything except in making the ear attuned to verbal music regret that it should not have been let alone.　To add elaborate notes to this lyric is like permeating lilies of the valley with analine dye.　It needs no rhyme.　So true is this that the hearer does not notice the lack of rhyme until his attention is called to it.　If rhyme is only an accompaniment to the form of poetry, not an essential part of that form, it might be well to inquire as to how far association is responsible for the impressions which rhythm gives us, — for if

[1] The Princess.

rhyme is dismissed we must use rhythm and
time as bases for the structure of verse-forms.
We all know that by a change of ictus the
solemn Welsh national air or the "Grosser
Gott" may be turned into a veritably jolly lilt.
And so, as Mr. Patmore says, his "Night and
Sleep" can be made a bacchanalian chorus by
another use of accent and silence. But if we
consider rhythm as a fixed quantity capable of
conveying definite impressions, we have only
to turn to the "Heathen Chinee" to find that
Bret Harte has, without changing an accent,
appropriated one of the most solemnly harmonious af Swinburne's measures in the
"Atalanta in Calydon." It is a far cry from
the "Heathen Chinee" to the finest of all
Swinburne's masterly experiments in metres;
but it is an example of an adaptation of dignity
to the antic mood,—and yet the sweep of sound
in the hymn in praise of Atalanta is not recalled
by the quaint complaint of the victim of the
bland Chinese. It is a parody, but the hearer
does not find it out until an accident or a remark by a previous discoverer informs him of
it. It probably would have remained unheeded
had not Mr. Bret Harte confessed his guilt.
The student of "Atalanta in Calydon" is
haunted by the resemblance, after it has been
pointed out; but to most of us the "Heathen
Chinee" could not have appeared in a more
natural or spontaneous form. It is not the
incongruity of the medium with the thought
that strikes us, for the *naiveté* of Bret Harte's
hero never was on sea or land; it is plainly

artificial; the meaning and the expression have
become one, and, by a process similar to that
of Rudyard Kipling, the author of the "Heathen Chinee" has added to our language a new
humorous verse-form which, though stolen
without detection, cannot be re-appropriated
without instant discovery.

The rhythm of—

> "Not with cleaving of shields
>   And their clash in thine ear
> Where the lord of fought fields.
>   Breaketh spearshaft from spear,
> Thou art broken, our lord, thou art broken,
>   With travail and labor and fear."

becomes, without change of accent, the chaunt
of Bret Harte's injured innocent.

> "Which is why I remark,
>   And my language is plain,
> That for ways that are dark,
>   And for tricks that are vain,
> The heathen Chinee is peculiar,
>   Which the same I am free to maintain.

> "In the scene that ensued
>   I did not take a hand;
> But the floor it was strewed
>   Like the leaves on the strand
> With the cards that Ah Sin had been hiding,
>   In the game 'he did not understand.'"

But there is, all the same, a difference, and
the difference lies, not in the rhythm, but in a
series of delicate, almost impalpable pauses
that change the character of the music. It is

in the management of the pauses, — in the
recognition of the value of time-beats, — that
Coventry Patmore's supremacy, in the Ode
form, lies.   In his "domestic verses" he uses
rhyme in places where Tennyson would not
have dreamed of it,—recklessly, audaciously;
but, in his highest moods, when his imagination is at its whitest heat, he treats rhyme as
an echo.   Why he retains it at all, except as a
concession to that conservatism which is the
perpetual foundation for his extremest radi-
calism, is an unanswered question.   As an
echo, not as a mere imitation of an echo, rhyme
has great musical possibilities which Mr. Patmore has only suggested.   Phrase answers to
phrase in music, but the effect is of strophe
complementing strophe, not of line answering
to line.   As in the sextette of a Petrarchan
sonnet, the rhymes echo one to the other
rather than boldly repeat the cadence with
equal voice, so rhyme, at its best is an echo,—
or, if a repetition, it is well softened by dis-
tance.   I speak of rhyme when applied to the
higher and finer moods of the mind.   As a help
to the expression of gaiety, high spirit, of the
intoxication of the senses, — as an assistance
to the "attack" of the vocalist, in songs written
for actual singing and full of the minor emotions, it is invaluable.   It would be only necessary to point to the "Nora Creina" of Tom
Moore to show this, if it needed to be
proven; it is to the brisker of his melodies
what the sound of the castinets is to
Spanish folk songs; absent, the loss would be

felt; but it is not an essential part of the melody.

The verse-form, — made up, in English, of catalexis, rhythm and rhyme, — addresses itself to the ear. The eye of late insists that verse shall consider it; but this demand is only a modern concession, entirely unreasonable, encouraged by the base education of the eye through the meretricious usurpations of the art of printing.

Now, who could or would sing or chaunt the every-day doings of Patmore's amiable lover and his lass without a loss of self-respect? Rhyme ought only to be a musical accompaniment. In the "Angel in the House" and "The Rosy Bosom'd Hours" it ceases to be a musical effect because it is ineffective and becomes merely an equivalent for the legend, "this is verse." "John Gilpin," a rhymed ballad, has the same right to exist as "Chevy Chase" or "Lord Bateman." Its recurrent rhymes might be crooned endlessly by an old nurse near a rural fireside. One of the principal uses of rhyme in the very old days was to put children to sleep,—Eve, no doubt, discovered that without recourse to psychology or physics. The author of Mother Goose's Melodies,—who is one of the greatest rhymsters in English,— found this out through no series of experiments, but through the intuitional wisdom of generations.

If rhyme is an aid to memory, let the primary text-books be in rhyme. As a relief to insomnia its value is unquestioned. All English poets since Shakespere have been safest, when, in long poems, they discarded it. The couplets of Pope tire us, if taken many at a time; and it is one of the greatest tributes to Dante, that his value has stood, among us English-speaking peoples, the test of rhymed translations.

As time goes on, poetry will be more and more addressed to the ear. It aims to express the inexpressible; it never succeeds because the inexpressible *is* inexpressible; but it approaches, it approximates; above all, it suggests. It flares or it glows, but it can never completely illuminate. Its form changes with the changes in speech and with the progress of the education of the people in music. When the people cease to find poetry musical, they let it alone. Old Fletcher of Saltoun's Wise Man spoke of the "ballads" of the people, not of verses in the modern sense. Wagner and the circle impressed, in various ways with the musical "time-spirit," have gradually modified the popular view of music in Western countries. It is now, even with the more cultured of the ignorant, not entirely a matter of melody. The popular ear is becoming more attuned to those delicate tones, compact of sound and silence, which makes up harmony. And verse music, which is a very different thing from music proper, is reflecting the effects of this progress. The difference exactly between verse and music can be tested only by physics. Sydney Lanier's researches, hypotheses, and experiment, founded greatly on Helmholtz, have taken off the chill that

this association might have given the advocates
of the traditional school of poetry. As Mr.
Edward Lucas White says: "We need to know
exactly what are the sounds used in music,
and exactly what are the sounds used in verse,
how far and in just what respects they differ.
Then we need to know to what degree each of
the characteristics of sound — namely: pitch,
time, loudness and quality — is of importance
in the makeup of the rhythm of verse; and the
like concerning music, and whether the importance of each in music is the same in respect
to the others as it is in verse. And when we
know all there is to know as to the differences
between the manners in which their characteristics are handled, we shall know all there is
to know about the difference between music
and verse, considering each as sound only.
Finally and definitely these questions can be
settled only by careful and well-devised laboratory experiments. In the absence of such
there is but a meagre and unsatisfactory basis
upon which to reason."[1]

This being true, exact conclusions as to
respective value of music and the musical
qualities of verse are at present out of our
reach; but there is no doubt that the effect
aimed at through verse is musical, and that
verse has, in common with music, rhythm,
time and what is called "quality." "Every
difference of quality," Mr. White says, in his

---

[1] On the Study of English Verse (unpublished). Edward
Lucas White.

interesting monograph, "is referable either to
the different sets of harmonics in the sounds
compared or to the harmonics which are loud
in one sound, being soft in the other, if the
series for each sound be the same." In music,
after time, pitch is of the greatest importance;
in verse, after time, quality is of the greatest
importance. In music there are combinations
that approach to rhyme; there is recurrence
approaching to parallelism in verse; — there
are constant repetitions of rythmical move-
ments, but not often repetitions of the last
note of a musical phrase exactly answering to
that vowel and consonantal combination which
we call rhyme. If there were no other reason,
this would be enough to show that rhyme cannot be judged by the analogy of music. But
to repeat, perhaps unwarrantably, verse has
no right to exist if it is not musical. To be
musical, it must have the vital qualities
of rhythm and time. Shakespere's sonnet
(LXXIII) is rhythmical; you can count the
time as easily as an orchestra leader wields his
baton to the notes of Chopin's funeral march.
Let us observe, though, that until we reach
the couplet the rhyme in this sonnet is not
forced upon us, as it is in the "domestic"
verses of Coventry Patmore. It is like a gentle
accompaniment; it does not force recurrent
sound upon us. The first quatrain of the octave
begins with a long, melancholy cadence:

"That time of year thou mayst in me behold
When yellow leaves, or none, or few, do hang
Upon those boughs which shake against the cold,
Bare, ruined choirs, were late the sweet birds sang."

In the second quatrain, the phrases become shorter, more personal, more emotional, more agitated:

> "In me thou see'st the twilight of such day
> As after sunset fadeth in the west;
> Which by and by black night doth take away,
> Death's second self, that seals up all in rest."

The rhyme in the sextette is not that mostly affected by Petrarch, who, in the most delicate of all forms, used it more carefully than either Sidney or Shakespere. The "crack of the whip," the couplet at the end of the sextette, almost spoils one of the most harmonious English sonnets we have, for suddenly the rhyme accompaniment makes itself heard in a disagreeable and epigrammatic jingle.

The phrases are again quick and short, breathed swiftly over the dying embers of the heart:

> "In me thou see'st the glowing of such fire,
> That on the ashes of his youth doth lie,
> As the death-bed whereon it must expire,
> Consumed with that which it was nourished by.
> This thou perceivest, which makes thy love more strong,
> To love that well which thou must leave ere long."

Here is verse-music in perfection, — time, rhythm, and even rhyme. It is delightful to the ear; and yet it is not more musical than the speech of Belarius (Cymbeline, Act IV, Scene II),

> "O thou goddess,
> Thou divine nature, how thyself thou blazon'st
> In these two princely boys! They are as gentle
> As zephyrs blowing below the violet,

> Not wagging his sweet head; and yet as rough,
> Their royal blood enchafed, as the rudest wind
> That by the top doth take the mountain pine,
> And make him stoop to the vale."

As Shakespere increases in power he disregards rhyme. In the early plays he dropped into rhyming couplets continually; his practice in the later days was in direct contrast. As he matures, he lays less stress on the end of a line, — a practice which shows that his ear had begun to lose the association of rhyme. Orlando's rhymes make easy mockery for Touchstone. And, after Ariel's

> "Hark, hark! I hear
> The strain of strutting chanticleer,
> Cry, cock-a-diddle-dow."

which the satirical spirit attunes to "Bow-wow," comes Prince Ferdinand's strain (Tempest, Act I, Scene II):

> "Where should this music be? I' th' air or th' earth?
> It sounds no more; and sure it waits upon
> Some god o' th' island. Sitting on a bank,
> Weeping again the king my father's wreck,
> This music crept by me upon the waters,
> Allaying both their fury and my passion
> With its sweet air; thence I have followed it,
> Or it had drawn me rather. But 'tis gone,
> No, it begins again."

Rhyme could not improve the harmony of Caliban's speech (Act III, Scene 2):

> "Be not afeard; the isle is full of noises,
> Sounds and sweet airs that give delight and hurt not.
> Sometimes a thousand twangling instruments
> Will hum about mine ears, and sometimes voices

That, if I then had waked after long sleep,
Will make me sleep again; and then, in dreaming,
The clouds methought would open, and show riches
Ready to drop upon me; that when I waked,
I cried to dream again."

The practice of Shakespere, — whose verse
music was always addressed to the ear, and
never to the eye, — shows that, in using the
noblest vehicle for imagination and thought
in our language,—the five-accented verse, with
the iambic quality predominant,— he avoided
rhyme. The practice of Coventry Patmore,
who consciously advanced the musical quality
of English verse many degrees, shows that, in
his best moments, he looked on rhyme as a
mere accessory.

The sonnet stands apart; its fourteen lines
are required, by rule, to have their bell-like
effect; but nothing is so like the couplet ending,—of which the English were so fond,—as
the clang of the typewriter's metals. The
sonnet was borrowed from a language which
rhymes naturally; in Italian it is easier to find
a rhyme than to avoid one. Take, at random,
the canzone, —

"Spirto gentil, che quelle membra reggi
Dentro alle qua' peregrinando alberga
Un signor valoroso, accorto, e saggio;
Poi che se' giunto all' onorata verga;
Con la qual Roma, e suoi erranti correggi,
E la richiamai al suo antico viaggio;
I' parlo a te, però ch'altrove un raggio
Non veggio di vertù, ch'al mondo e spenta;
Nè trovo chi di mal far si vergogna."
                (Rime del Petrarca, Canzone XI).

In English this richness cannot be attained by the most stringent labor. There is too much noise in our words, and, in proportion, very little music. In the sonnet, artifice must be so chastened that it attains the supremest technical effects of art, — ease and simplicity. The thought of the octave may flow, wavelike, into the third quatrain, if you like the English form; or it may, if you prefer Petrarch's way, be closely allied to the syllogism, with the marked change from the premises to the conclusion. Like a diamond of fourteen facets, it must be cut and polished until it is lucent, in every part; there must be no flaw, and Petrarch and those before him insisted that rhymes—the *sonnetti*—must ring at intervals; but the Italians, who kick a rhyme with every step they take, would not stoop to pick up too many, while the earlier English made great and awkward strides in pursuit of rhymes which are very coy in our language. An unrhymed sonnet is impossible, for the conquest of the form is in proportion to the arbitrary difficulty overcome; it is a thing apart — *sui generis*. And it is so written that the echoes of the mandolin—or, in great hands,—of the harp must accompany the sonnet. Otherwise, it could not be as Italian masters made it. It is an exotic form torn from a richer soil yet flourishing among us. But the ode is natural to us. It is a form of inspiration, in which every palpitation of the great thought is seen beneath the drapery of words. The English language is opulent in odes, from Spenser's

Epithalamium to Lowell's "Commemoration."
From Milton's "Lycidas" to Gilder's "I am
the Spirit of the Morning Sea," they circle in
splendor. And in this innermost splendor
glow the Odes of Coventry Patmore. Crashaw
had his gleams of great light. He came near
to the nimbus of St. Teresa and the halo of
St. John the Divine; but Patmore is nearer.
It was reserved for him, too, to atone for the
tinkling of "The Angel in the House" and
"The Rosy Bosom'd Hours" by boldly restor-
ing to English verse its heritage of music.
Patmore does not disregard rhyme in his
"Odes," but it becomes an echo; he uses it as
the servant of his thought; with him it is not
like the genius of the Arabian tales, escaped
from its vase, and tyrannous. He begins the
work of emancipation by "rhyming at indefi-
nite intervals." "A license," he says, somewhat frightened by this radical change from
his earlier habit, "which is counterbalanced,
in the writings of all poets who have employed
this metre (catalectic verse) successfully by
unusual frequency in the recurrence of the
same rhyme."[1]

In "The Unknown Eros," Mr. Patmore
propounds his theory and shows how it works
in experiment. A poet, as a rule, gets the
music in his head and measures it afterwards.
"So," says Mr. White, "no one imagines that
Barye had any lack of imagination because,
after he had modeled, say a group of animals

---

[1] Poems, by Coventry Patmore: Fifth Collective Edition.
London, 1894. George Bell & Sons.

in violent action, he went over the model using a pantographic device when he was not modeling life size, and measured every part of the model to see if his eye had been at fault anywhere." And the poet uses his "pantographic device," his rules and measures, his tests and analyses, after the wildwood notes of his song have come to him. It may not be altogether a "wildwood" song, for by some unknown and unconscious process he has taken from the wind and thunder and the sea sounds their fundamental tones and harmonies. When and how did the song rise in his heart? Who knows? Maurice de Guérin's "Centaure" well exclaims: "Les mortels qui touchèrent les dieux par leur vertu ont reçu de leur mains des lyres pour charmer les peuples,—mais rien de leur bouche inexorable."

Coventry Patmore's music was deliberately composed by him, on hints found in the poets, from Drummond of Hawthornden to our own time, who had made "some of the noblest flights of English poetry." He restores silence to the singer, for his "catalexis" is only silence filled by the beating of time. He enables the student who could not find the law of the "Ode" among the many lawless imitations of Pindar, to touch a standard by which the finest form of the lyric may be judged. "In its highest order, the lyric or 'ode,'" he says, "is a tetrameter, the line having the time of eight iambics. When it descends to narrative or the expression of a less exalted strain of thought, it becomes a dimeter, with the time of four; and it is allowable to vary the tetrameter 'ode' by the introduction of passages in either or both of these inferior measures; but not, I think, by the use of any other."[1]

'The though, however,' he assumes, "must voluntary move harmonious numbers." He demands that final pauses be considered. He lays down as a great general law that *the elementary measure, or integer, of English verse is double the measure of ordinary prose,* — that is to say it is the space which is bounded by alternate accents; *that every verse proper contains two, three, or four of these 'metres,'* or as with a little allowance they may be called 'dipodes,' *and that there is properly no such thing as hypercatalexis.* All English verses in common cadence are therefore dimeters, trimeters, or tetrameters, and consist, when they are *full,* i. e., without catalexis, of eight, twelve, or sixteen syllables. Verses in triple cadence obey the same law, only their length exceeds that of the trimeter on account of the great number of syllables or places for syllables (twenty-four) which would be involved in the tetrameter of such a cadence."

While admitting, or rather insisting, that time and rhythm are the necessities of verse-music, he declares, almost with solemnity, that rhyme and alliteration—"head rhyme"— are no mere ornaments; the former marks essential metrical pauses, the latter "is a very effective mode of conferring emphasis on the accent which is the primary foundation of

---

[1] The Unknown Eros: preface to 8d edition.

metre."[1] This assertion is not, however, cor-
roborated in the series of "Odes" which gives
Mr. Patmore an unique place among English-
writing poets. These great lyrics do not, in
form, fit all parts of his theory. They cannot
be justified by the old foot-rule methods of
scansion; they are admirable material for the
study of metres, and they seem to indicate
that the verse of the future must have that
spontaneity,—exclusive of monotony,—which
all beautiful things have. His famous narra-
tive-lyric, "The Toys," is, by comparison, the
severest criticism upon the verses on which his
earlier reputation rested. No man with a
sense of humor could have written most of
them, and their method seems to justify the
impression that he had to revolt against them,
or perish as a poet. The quality of spontaneity
and the characteristic of plasticity are evident
in all those nobler lyrics. They answer to all
the definitions of poetry and still have that
hidden principle which no definition covers,
and is felt, but which never has even been
fully described. The "Ode" that of all in
"The Unknown Eros," best exemplifies Mr.
Patmore's theories, and in which his inspiration is complete, is the seventh, "To the
Body." It opens with the sweeping phrase,

"Creation and Creator's crowning good."

It is like the full tide of the first movement of
a symphony; it gives the time and the scope
of the piece. He mars the effect when he attempts to rhyme "good" with "infinitude,"—

[1] Essay on English Metrical Law.

> "Wall of infinitude;
> Foundation of the sky,
> In Heaven forecast
> And longed for from eternity,
> Though laid the last;
> Reverberating dome
> Of music cunningly built home
> Against the void and idolent disgrace
> Of unresponsive space;
> Little sequestered pleasure-house
> For God and for His Spouse."

This is dignified; this is solemn; it is pitched in the highest plane of aspiration; it will bear any analysis based on Mr. Patmore's theory of catalexis; but, if verse is addressed to the 'ear, why should that conservative rhyme for "sky," "eternity," be addressed to the eye? There are reasons of convenience and conventionality for his dividing his verse into lines which are only parts of a single musical phrase. For example,—

> "Elaborately, yea, past conceiving fair,
> Since from the graced decorum of the hair,
> Ev'n to the tingling sweet
> Soles of the simple, earth-confiding feet,
> And from the inmost heart
> Outwards unto the thin
> Silk curtain of the skin,
> Every least part
> Astonished hears
> And sweet replies to some like region of the spheres."

Here we have an arrangement of musical phrases, dependent entirely on cunningly distributed silences, filled with time-beats. These

phrases are *grave* or *allegretto*, as the sentiment
dictating to the plastic form, forces them;
but, where the rhyme does not show that a
line ends, there is not, except it be a stopt-
ending, any indication of the line, to the ear.

> "Formed for a dignity prophets but darkly name,
> Lest shameless men cry 'Shame.'
> So rich with wealth concealed
> That Heaven and Hell fight chiefly for this field;
> Clinging to everything that pleases thee
> With indefectible fidelity;
> Alas, so true
> To all thy friendships that no grace
> Thee from thy sin can wholly disembrace;
> Which thus 'bides with thee as the Jesubite,
> That, maugre all God's promises could do,
> The chosen people never conquer'd quite;
> Who therefore lived with them,
> And that by formal truce and as of right,
> In metropolitan Jerusalem."

The music of the sustained phrase reaches the
culmination in

> "For which false fealty
> Thou must needs, for a season, lie
> In the grave's arms, foul and unshriven,
> Albeit in Heaven,
> Thy crimson-throbbing Glow
> Into its old abode aye pants to go,
> And does with envy see
> Enoch, Elijah, and the Lady, she
> Who left the roses in her body's lieu."

There are those that hold that the passionate,
yet solemn music at the close, defies Mr. Patmore's rules. The fact remains that it is pure

verse music. Tried by the tests drawn from
the Greek and Latin, which so far as English
metres are concerned, are alien to us, these
fine harmonic phrases would be rejected; the
time has gone when the music in our language
must be stifled to suit outworn rhetorical
measures applied to it.

> "O, if the pleasure I have known in thee
> But my poor faith's poor first-fruits be,
> What quintessential, keen, ethereal bliss
> Then shall be his
> Who has thy birth-time's consecrating dew
> For death's sweet chrism retain'd,
> Quick, tender, virginal, and unprofaned!"

It is to be regretted that the exquisite sense
which caught and gave this musical sequence
should have marred it for the ear by making
'his' read 'hiss'. It would have been better
to have done without the rhyme.

In the little pathetic sonata, "If I Were
Dead", which manifests the results of his
theories, Mr. Patmore uses rhyme with an
audacity which seems lawless; — fortunately
one forgets this in the admirable effect pro-
duced by accent and pauses, so managed that
silences seem as the shadow of waving
leaves, —

> "If I were dead, you'd sometimes say, 'Poor Child'.
> The dear lips quivered as they spake,
> And the tears brake,
> From eyes which, not to grieve me, brightly smiled.
> · Poor Child, poor Child!
> I seem to hear your laugh, your talk, your song.
> It is not true that Love will do no wrong.
> Poor Child!

And did you think when you so cried and smiled,
How I, in lonely nights, should lie awake,
And of those words your full avengers make?
Poor Child, poor Child!
And now, unless it be
That sweet amends thrice told are come to thee,
O God, have thou no mercy upon me!
Poor Child!

"Wind and Wave" opens with,

"The wedded light and heat,
Winnowing the witless space
Without a let,
What are they till they beat
Against the sleepy sod, and there beget
Perchance the violet, —"

and drifts into silence with

"And so the whole
Unfathomable and immense
Triumphing tide comes at the last to reach
And bursts in wind-kissed splendors on the deaf'ning
Where forms of children in first innocence   [beach,
Laugh and fling pebbles on the rainbow'd crest
Of its untired unrest."

The place of "The Unknown Eros," and
the other poems which are catalectic, is fixed.
There can be no question as to their position
among the best poems in English speech.
They are worth much, from the technical
point of view, because, — whether Mr. Patmore's theories stand or not,—he has applied
a new measure, — or newly discovered an old
measure,—which opens wider vistas of delight
to all whose ear is attuned to sounds of beauty.

Without the intention of doing so, he shows us that rhyme is practically unimportant. Unconsciously, too, he offers evidence against artificial conventions, and at the same time proves that the "exact science of verse" is a vain phrase until the value of speech sounds be settled by physics. A time may come when we shall not entirely agree with Sidney Lanier, in the last chapter of "The Science of English Verse" that: "For the artist in verse there is no law; the perception and love of beauty constitute the whole outfit; and what is herein set forth is to be taken merely as enlarging that perception and exalting that love." But we shall always hold that "in all cases the appeal is to the ear; *but the ear should, for that purpose, be educated up to the highest plane of culture.*" The sense so refined makes for law.

The "Odes" of Coventry Patmore are precious for this sort of culture. They may lead to greater and more splendid forms of utterance in the future than either Shakespere or Milton caught and gave forth. The day has not come when the reading of poetry will be taught as carefully as the musician teaches the reading of music, but a score of the verse effects of Mr. Patmore might easily be prepared, within certain musical limitations, which would broaden the views of those readers of poetry who now fancy that the music of the great poet consists principally in recurrent rhymes or assonances, and thus limit their perception and enjoyment.

THIS is an age of the revival of philosophies, and these philosophies are expressed through literature. The form of literature which at present dominates the greater part of the reading world is the novel. It has become a handbook of philosophy, and nearly every novelist feels that he is unworthy of his avocation if he cannot find a philosophical theory for his practice.

The French critics, who have exquisitely refined the tools of their trade, are largely responsible for this; and M. Brunetière, who is a Darwinian, but not a "naturalist," is using the material offered by the novel as a great part in his work of showing that literature is both a theory and an art. He is fond of the word "evolution," but he is keen and broad-minded enough to see that literature is not science, though the causes which lead to its creation may be treated in a philosophical manner. In spite of the passion of his nation for analysis, his methods are synthetical. As M. Jules Lemaître says:[1] "M. Brunetière est incapable, ce semble, de considérer une œuvre, quelle qu'elle soit, grande ou petite, sinon dans

---

[1] Les Contemporains (sexième série.)

ses rapports avec un groupe d'autres œuvres,
dont la relation avec d'autres groupes, à tra-
vers le temps et l'espace, lui apparaît immé-
diatement, et aussi de suite."

The power of doing this,—and nobody who
knows M. Brunetière's work can deny that he
does it admirably, — implies the possession of
an enormous amount of territory, from whose
fastnesses he can draw at will. This territory
he has conquered thoroughly; he has examined
every acre and even yard of it most minutely;
and in the splendor of his conquest and his
use of it, he is superior to those great critics that
preceded him, — Sainte Beuve and Edmond
Scherer. If one, however, applies his synthetical method to his position as a critic, one at
first thought groups with him two authors
who, at a second glance, seem to have little
resemblance to him. And these are Louis
Veuillot and W. H. Mallock. And, applying
to him, too, his theory of evolution, we discover, with hope, that the result of Sainte
Beuve and Scherer and a great group of lesser
critics is a man who, in is desire for "a principle of authority has been led on various occasions to make concessions to Catholicity, which
may very well seem excessive."[1] Brunetière
is hardly a Neo-Catholic, he is not less of a
Pessimist than he was, and it is a question
whether he does not hold Buddhism[2] as of at
least equal value with Christianity, yet it is

---

[1] Irving Babbett: Atlantic Monthly, June, 1897.

[2] La Philosophie de Schopenhauer: Questions de Cri-
tique: 1886.

consoling to know that, while the apostles of
science and work and the preachers of aes-
theticism and idleness place annihilation as
their conclusion, a logical and great critic
looks with longing, but as yet perhaps without
solace, to the one religion of infallible authority. M. Anatole France, who is M. Rénan
bathed in extract of violets, would prefer the
Paradise of Mohammed; M. Brunetière looks
forward to a Nirvâna, but he cannot accept
the quiescent state and the absence of the karma,—for him soul-activity will never cease;
he is too practical for mysticism, too scholastic
for impressionism. As a logician who halts,
he is like Mallock; as a dogmatist who will not
tolerate unreason, he is like Veuillot; hence
his "concessions," hence his problems. The
sarcasm and invective of Louis Veuillot against
the schools of philosophy in letters that he
detested were not much more fierce than are
the attacks of Brunetière on the "scientific
naturalistic" school. His evolution is in progress, and it is evident that the Darwinian
who finds, the older he grows, the need for a
solid philosophical and moral background for
his science and art, is gradually losing his
respect for Schopenhauer and his tendency to
regard Christianity and Buddhism with equal
sympathy. The man who refused to calum-
niate the Middle Ages and accused the writers
of the eighteenth century of having invented
their darkness has not been slow to discover
that the abuse of Darwinism and the teaching

of Schopenhauer have helped to produce the manifestations he most abhors in literature.

It is remarkable that England and America, while they show us the results of the philosophical tendencies in literature, offer such a small amount of serious criticism. The seeker who would analyze the influences that make partisans of thought must turn to the French, who have a way of settling questions without circumlocution. Besides, in France art is a religion, and while the artist there takes himself seriously, the artist in other countries — always excepting the German musician, — wastes a good deal of his mental force in trying to believe that he is serious. Consequently, French literary art dominates the form of expression which, for want of a better name, we call the novel. The march of events and the complexity of modern life have become so sublime and amazing, that Melchior de Vogüé expresses a truth we all know when he says of the progress of Germany: "It would require a Shakespere, doubled by a Montesquieu to describe the life of this country during the last three years." Similarly the life of all civilized countries, as depicted in history—which, when not a mere collection of annals, is as personal as fiction—requires that the author should be something more than a lyrical romancer. There must be in him a stronger element than the mere desire to chaunt or to recite great events. As depicted in the novel, which is not only the history of the mind, but the essentials from which the historian must, in the future, draw much of his material, life is no longer a mere spectacle, with red fire flaming here and there and the torch-bearing Hymen at the end. Whether it is well that a form of expression, which was gay at times, more often at least cheerful and always exciting, should have become a vehicle for the consideration of all sorts of problems, is not the question at present. But in no age has the art of fiction received such careful attention and analysis. Even in England where, in Miss Austin's time, the novel was dropped behind the sofa or the sideboard when visitors came and a compilation of sermons immediately taken up, it has been, for at least fifty years, the favorite tool of men who wished either to construct or destroy. Newman, Wiseman, Lord Beaconsfield, Charles Kingsley, Carlyle— all resorted to fiction; and no doubt a posthumous novel by Mr. Gladstone will be discovered, since this is the only form of thought expression he seems so far to have neglected.

M. Brunetière, while crediting Protestantism with the morality of the English novel,[1] declares that in France the novel serves as a destructive force to batter uncomfortable institutions or to attack unpleasant persons, but that he doubts whether it will ever become, as in the hands of Dickens, Thackeray, and George Eliot, an instrument for higher things.

---

[1] "C'est ainsi qu'il manquera probablement toujours au naturalisme français ce que trois siècles de forte education protestante ont infusé de valeur morale au naturalisme anglais."—Le Roman Naturaliste, p. 241.

He notes the distinction between the moral
teaching of George Eliot — "the moral of the
good bad books"—and the morality of Thackeray, which is insupportably preachy, narrow
and prudhommesque." She teaches the morality of Herbert Spencer; "there is no higher
morality," Brunetière says, "none more Uto-
pian;" and he compares it, with gentle scorn,
to the morality of Madame Craven and Miss
Yonge.

For serious criticism of literature one must
go to France, where literary manifestations
are not only considered from the point of view
of art, but from the point of view of philosophy: but even M. Brunetière, whom some of
us Catholics have adopted with enthusiasm,
perhaps a little too ardent, does not, as a rule,
take that view of morality of which we approve.
We love him most reasonably for his hatreds;
—we find at the end of the century a critic
making the same fight against false philosophy
in literature that Veuillot and Brownson made,
with a much greater power of having himself
heard. We cannot help seeing, from the example of M. Brunetière, that a serious student
of literature must devote great attention to the
development and scientific causes of the novel,
but that, in so doing, he finds himself helpless
unless he can know some fixed standard of
philosophy, morality, and art to which to appeal. The present intellectual position of M.
Brunetière is due to this fact: he must accept
the theories of the "impressionists," like MM.
Anatole France and Jules Lemaître, grope

along until he finds a basis which will be popular and still have a "scientific" appearance or
admit that the absolute exists, and that the
absolute, the ultimate tribune, is God. M.
Brunetière and the schools of critics about
him are living proofs that art cannot live for
art alone, nor science for science alone, and
that the very denial of God and dogma is
essentially an affirmation.

Psychology will some day or other give us
the key to what we call temperament. Until
then we shall be forced to listen to endless
theories on the consciousness and intentions of
Shakespere and to hear the modern doers of
various kinds of work wasting many words in
striving to justify the result of natural bent,
early training, and the demands of their time
upon them, by formulating philosophies for it
all. M. Zola, not admitting the manifest truth
that he took advantage of the popularization
of science in order to make an effect which
accorded with his natural tendency, invents a
philosophy of "scientific naturalism." Carlyle,
who invented a style for the purpose of effect,
too, and took advantage of dyspepsia in order
to accent it, might, had the process been in
fashion in his time, have made a scientific
apology for himself in much the same way.
But he was of his times. M. Zola, in attempt-
ing to be effective, was, he thought, obliged to
be coarse and incorrect in his style; to be
heard, too, he must make a sensation, and
grovel in the filth at the feet of the people.
Unconsciously, he was following a tendency

which forced Hugo to be violent and truculent
in his protest against aristocratic classicism, to
commit brutal acts in his dramas; for it is
certain that when literary art in France "appeals directly to the people — being innately
cultivated, chiselled, exquisite, in a word,
aristocratic,—it becomes exceedingly coarse,
declamatory and incorrect."[1]

M. Zola will admit no force unknown to
him in his method, though we know he finds
room somewhere for his guess at heredity.
Yet, if he were a true analyst, he would see
that the reaction from classicism in his own
case is only romantic after all. While M. Zola
shrieks, like Caliban, at scholasticism, he is
forced to give a metaphysical reason for his
nastiness, just as modern poets often feel themselves obliged, out of consideration for science,
to explain their involuntary rhythms by an
elaborate appeal to physics. In fact, he is
forced by the demand that everything shall be
referred to philosophy, whether divine or not,
to flee for dignity to the thing he most detests.
He is like an actor hating all things classical,
who would attempt to increase his height
when topped with a tall hat, by shoeing himself with the cothurnus!

Having written a certain number of novels,
founded on a hypothesis which attracted him,
he now goes forth in search of a philosophy.
The syllogism, the soul of scholasticism, haunts
him, as it haunts every other man brought up

---

[1] "Le Roman Naturaliste," p. 242. La théorie de l'art
pour l'art est essentiellement latine.

in scholastic methods. He wrote "Le Rêve" in order to show that he could be moral and "chaste." It was a conscious effort; he went against his tendencies, and he pointed to it with pride. It was even more difficult to find a philosophy which would explain him, not as a mere writer, an intuitive observer, a magical expressor, but as a scientist. It is necessary to accentuate this here in order to show that the position of the novel and the novelist has entirely changed in the last fifty years. It has become something that must be reckoned with and which deserves as much study as any other great social phenomenon.

Science and work are the key-words of M. Zola's system. From his experimental philosophy he gets these axioms: "Man must be scientific; man must work." Tolstoï, who also arranges his various philosophies in the form of novels, comments on this, from his point of view, in 1884: "The most part of what is called religion," he says, "is only the superstition of the past; the most part of what is called science is only the superstition of the present." Tolstoï goes on to say that even before he heard Zola's formula given to the youth of France, he was surprised at the fixed impression, above all in Europe, that work is a species of virtue. "I had always believed it was pardonable only in a being deprived of reason, as the ant in the fable, to elevate work to the rank of a virtue and to glory in it. M. Zola is sure that work makes man good. I have always remarked the con-

trary." Work, even when it is not entirely
selfish,—he continues—"work for work's sake,
makes men, as well as ants, hard and cruel.
"Even if work be not a vice, it can not, from
any point of view, be regarded as a merit."[1]

One observes a great difference between the
teachings of Zola and those of Count Tolstoï,
both eminent writers of the modern hand-
books of philosophy. With one, religion is a
superstition and science a living light; with the
other both are largely superstitions. Authors
like Sir Walter Scott and Manzoni, believed
that their work was to illuminate life rather
than to explain it.

If M. Zola claimed only to be a teller of tales
and said frankly that he "wallowed" because
there are many persons who find his wallowing
interesting enough to be paid for, we should
have no concern with him here. If M. Brunetière treated literature,—and the literature of
the novel particularly, — only as a means of
producing effects, his critical studies would
have no claim on attention in this paper. But
both these gentlemen turn irresistibly from the
modus of their work to its philosophy, and
draw from it ethical conclusions. M. Brunetière, logically following his method, must
come in time to see that a system of ethics
which can be preached with confidence must
have an infallible foundation. M. Zola, following his method as logically as he can, will
never end by turning the impossible into the

---

[1] Zola, Dumas, Guy de Maupassant; Leo Tolstoï. Translated into French by E. Halpérine-Kalminsky.

possible. To make processes which go on in the soul as evident as those in the lungs of a cat are to the eyes of an experimenting surgeon the soul must be touched by a steel scalpel.

The chief experimental scientific novelist, who is M. Zola, breathed jubilantly when he discovered Claude Bernard's "Introduction to the Study of Experimental Medicine." He had at last a standard to which he could mould his own. Bernard holds that the spontaneity of living bodies is not opposed to the employment of experiment.[1] "The end of all experimental method, the boundary of all scientific research, is thus identical for living and for inanimate bodies; it consists in finding the motions which unite a phenomenon of any kind to its nearest cause, or, in other words, in determining the conditions necessary for the manifestation of this phenomenon." He has no hope of ever finding the "why" of things; he can only know the "how." "The experimental novel is a consequence of the scientific evolution of the century." M. Zola says: "It continues and completes physiology, which itself leans for support on chemistry and medicine; it substitutes for the study of the abstract metaphysical man the study of the natural man, governed by physical and chemical laws, and modified by the influence of his surroundings; it is, in one word, the literature of our scientific age, as the classical and ro-

---

[1] Bernard as quoted by Zola, in "The Experimental Novel," translated by Belle M. Sherman.

mantic literature corresponded to a scholastic
and theological age."

It would be useless to give so much space to
M. Zola's "determinism," if he were the only
exponent of it. Fallacious as it seems to men
of faith, to men who hold firmly to the supernatural, it has a specious quality of insinuation
for folk of unfixed principle, whether it be
covered by Grant Allen's Hedonism or Hardy's
Pessimism; in a phrase, almost any jargon
may pass if it be concealed by that blanket
word—scientific.

The experimental scientific novelist is a
student of diseases. He takes the body in the
clinic and cuts into the ulcer; he will not per-
mit his disciples to smoke a cigar in his dissect-
ing room,—it might create an illusion, and all
palliative illusions are idealistic! Idealism is
the enemy. "Let us compare, for one instant,
the work of the idealistic novelist to ours," M.
Zola says, "and here this word idealistic refers
to writers who cast aside observation and experiment and base their works on the supernatural and irrational, who admit, in a word,
the power of mysterious forces outside of the
determinism of the phenomenon."

The author who admits the supernatural is
as odious to the "scientific experimentalists"
as is the vivisector who believes in a soul which
he cannot see or touch. The "scientific experimentalist" is a doctor of letters, whose
occupation is gone when health reigns. Nevertheless, the novelist who places himself before
his subject on the table of the clinic must have

an idea. Readers of M. Zola will naturally
wonder in what way this personal idea or
hypothesis differs from the "theory" of the
idealistic novelist; he does not answer this
question. Jules Verne, whom the superior
"scientific experimentalist" doubtless holds
to be rather frivolous, occurs to one's mind in
glancing at this elaborate exposition; he has
ideas; he uses them as search lights to find
strange combinations of facts in his imagination, and no doubt he will be quite willing to
accept these combinations as truths if they are
ever proved. The naturalistic experimental
novelist would treat the story of Lancelot and
Guinevere in this way: First, there is the idea,
which is, that in an effete state of society,
where idealism is rampant, sin is supposed to
exist. King Arthur, Guinevere, Lancelot, are
combinations of phosphorus, oxygen, nitrogen
and whatever else chemistry finds them to be.
Arthur does not count; the experimental scientific novelist could hardly deal with him; Lancelot and Guinevere follow certain inevitable
physiological laws. Tainted with idealism, they
fancy that they sin, not knowing that the experimental novelist has effaced sin. The
consequence is that the consciousness of sin,
which is "scientifically" impossible, produces
a false and morbid condition in the whole
Round Table, and the poor creatures, who had
not even read Paul Bert's nice little scientific
primer, die miserable deaths in convent cells,
sacrificed to idealism. Hamlet might be treated
in a similar manner,—the hallucination of the

old-fashioned ghost on the subject of the "sins done in his days of nature" being the disease for the experimental treatment of the scientist.

But may any process be scientific, the results of which can not be verified? May any method be scientific which can be applied only by one man? The Keely Motor may be to us magic or charlatanism; if it be clearly explained, so that its processes can be squared with natural laws; if experts can repeat its processes, it becomes scientific, and ceases to be "magical."

It is plain that the creation of a novelist or a poet can never belong to science. Let us presume that you find your Becky Sharp, — exactly like *your* conception of Thackeray's intriguer, — are you sure that she is really *his* Becky Sharp? *You* may think she is. In the processes of physics, chemistry and physiology, experimentalism is not founded on your thought or mine. Literature is compact of imagination. Imagination may be the prophet of science, but it is not science; it can never be science; it soars beyond what the experimentalist calls the rational. Mr. Coventry Patmore puts it,—"The more lofty, living and spiritual the intellect and character become, the more is need perceived for the sap of life which can only be sucked from the inscrutable and, to the wholly rational mind, repulsive ultimates of nature and instinct."[1] The experimental scientific novelist either ignores this truth or treats it as an aberration. Some men—a few—are born with their hearts on the

[1] Religio Poetae, p. 128.

right side. They are abnormal; they answer,
in the opinion of the gentlemen of this school,
to the idealist in life and letters. The idealist
has lived for many centuries; the scientific
novelist's mission is to exterminate him, and
the scientific experimentalist "is always a little
Atlas who goes[2] stumbling along with his eye-
balls bursting from his head under his self-
imposed burden." It is a merciful thing that
he does not discover that the world he thinks
he holds has become only a goitre under his
chin, which, unhappily, does not stop the
action of his jaws.

That M. Zola's philosophy is taken seriously
in France, M. Brunetière's fulminations show,
— and M. Brunetière has kept them up for a
long time. That there are many cultivated
persons who believe that criticism may exist
without canons, the success of M. Anatole
France and M. Jules Lemaître shows, — and
M. Anatole France and M. Jules Lemaître
have been writing for a long time. M. Zola
is bewildered by Darwin, and he seizes Claude
Bernard as the raft to which he clings in a sea
of inconsistent romance. When he discovers
that the raft is water-logged, he will grasp the
later support offered by the dictum of M. Le
Dantec,—that beyond the laws of physics and
chemistry there is nothing affecting the senses
of living, observing beings, transcending the
laws governing gross matter, and, he will add,
there can be nothing. MM. France and Lemaître have not even the decency of pretend-

---

[2] Ibid.

ing to reverence science. "I am sure only of my impressions," M. Lemaître says. M. Gaston Deschamps, who has brilliancy and common sense, laughs a little at them both, while gravely remarking that Guy de Maupassant, though not "a philosopher by profession, was saturated with philosophy and science."[8] Always partridges—and philosophy!

Critics of the type of M. Brunetière are rare in England and our own country. There are Saintsbury and Dowden; there are Stedman, Richard H. Stoddard, Howells, Hazeltine and Irving Babbett. They do not seem to be so serious as their French colleagues, perhaps because their work is not looked upon nationally as great or important. Of these Mr. Howells is most colored, both in his creative and analytical products, by the modern French. He is a naturalist, too,—but he confines himself to the nerves; he is a specialist in slight nervous difficulties. Nobody of taste can deny his charm, which is strongest when he forgets the theory that realism, of a decent sort, is to regenerate the world.

The haste with which books are reviewed prevents grave and careful criticism; and most of our reviewers are, from defects in philosophical training and lack of time, only impressionists of the sketchest kind. It ought to be remembered that books go on living, for good or ill, years and years after they are forgotten by the critics. They disappear and be-

---

[8] La vie et les livres: Gaston Deschamps.

come white paper again, but their seeds remain and germinate forever and forever.

The English, whose taste in novels largely dominates ours, have borrowed from France the idea of making their works of fiction into tremendously philosophical treatises. In fact, the French schools, to which we owe the later Henry James[1] and the methods of Harold Frederic,[2] have permeated Hardy and Meredith, Mrs. Humphrey Ward, and half a dozen others.

It is difficult to account for Miss Marie Corelli; she was, no doubt, struck out of the brain of a mahatma by a flaming comet.

Pessimism and evolution and experimental naturalism are apparent, more or less, in all. Even Stevenson does not concern himself with God and the supernatural motive. "The naturalistic writer," says M. Zola,[3] "believes that there is no necessity to pronounce on the question of God. He is a creative force, and that is all. Without entering into a discussion as to the subject of this force, without wishing still further to specify it, he takes nature from the beginning and analyzes it. His work is the same as that of our chemists and physicists. He but gathers together and classifies the data, without ever referring them to a common standard, without drawing conclusions about the ideal." It seems like a blunder, — which in literary criticism means a crime against

---

[1] The Experimental Novel, p. 401.

[2] The Awkward Age.

[3] The Damnation of Theron Ware.

good taste, — to intimate that the adorable
Stevenson should be submitted to analysis.
There can be no question that Miss Wedgewood is right when she calls him "non-
moral";[1] she is just, too, when she points out
the fact that between the direct moral tone of
George Eliot, for all her Herbert Spencerism,
and Stevenson and Meredith, there is a marked
difference. Meredith, the chief novelist of
our time, is an "experimentalist"; he chooses
his subjects and tries to produce re-actions.
God may exist "as a creative force," but
Meredith has not found it, necessary to consider that. Diana of the Causeways, Lord
Ormont's Aminta, the persons in "Richard
Feveril," are treated as a demonstrator of
anatomy handles his bones, — and the experimental lecturer makes epigrams that have
light, but no warmth. The philosophy of
Meredith is Epicureanism restrained in expression by the reticence of a distinguished patri-
cian of letters. And neither in "Marius the
Epicurian" nor in "Gaston de Latour" can
Pater conceal in his art the trail of the bad old
philosophy.

The text on which Mr. Hardy seems to have
based the philosophy of his latest works is
from Schopenhauer: "There are two things
which make it impossible to believe that this
world is the successful work of an all-wise, all-
good and, at the same time, all-powerful Being.
First, the misery which abounds in it every-

---

[1] Ethics and Literature. Julia Wedgewood. Contempo-
rary Review for January, 1897.

where; and, second, the obvious imperfection of its highest product, man, who is a burlesque on all he should be."

If Mr. Hardy were an actual realist, not a . mere experimentalist, the world would be only a spring-board from which his creatures ought to plunge into a sea of nothingness. And he, doubtless disagreeing with Schopenhauer in regarding suicide as unjustifiable, should not to be hard-hearted enough to expect them to live under the hopelessness which he has heaped upon them. Life is bad, sad, he teaches us; women are young and we imagine they are beautiful, but the allure is only that a man be snared into marriage and be unhappy ever afterward. Nature is fair and cruel, and everywhere suggestive of the worship of Phallas; and what matters it all!

Hardy and Meredith are consummate artists, and nobody will refuse that adjective to Stevenson's art. But let us remark, in all coldness, without partisanship, if necessary, that in the nineteenth century after the birth of Christ, the false philosophies of the vanished world again appear, and the intellectual and cultivated Christians of our time receive them without much question, with no apologies, with no protest, under the form most insidious, most permeating. With Stevenson life is a problem, for which he has no solution. To live bravely, not thinking of the end, is his motto. The slightest hurt to the smallest creature is, in his code, more terrible than the pride of Lucifer. Men and women are good and bad as they have

been made good or bad; theit souls may not
exist as souls, but their karma—the essence of
their acts influenced by the acts of their ancestors—exists, and it determines their earthly
fate. Stevenson has more skill than Sir Walter
Scott; he, like Hardy and George Meredith,
can tell a story better than Cervantes. Le Sage
and Fielding and Manzoni are bunglers in
their art compared to these new men. But
there is nothing predicting that they will live
as Hamlet and "Promessi Sposi," "The Bride
of Lammermoor" and "The Newcomes" and
"Adam Bede" will live. Even the fundamental passions fail of effect if there are no
gods to whom to appeal. Persephone in
Hades is not a fit subject for poetry, with
Jupiter dead and no golden harvest and no
blue flowers in the corn above her, bathed in
the sunshine, for which she longs. Heine's
yearning pine is naught without the splendid
vision of the sun-flooded land of the palm.
There are no finer artists in words than Flaubert and De Maupassant and Meredith and
Hardy and Stevenson; we may admire the
carving of the statue of Mercury without burn-
ing incense to the cult it represents. But,
while the art is fine, there is a lack of depth
beyond it; the sea of eternity sends no winds
to the land where its creatures live. They
pretend not to have heard that Pan is dead or
that the Galilean has conquered.

Mrs. Humphrey Ward is a professional
philosopher. She teaches consciously; she
analyzes persons in order to construct others.

She is a "modern," too, an experimentalist,
a scientist; her human interest saves her
in spite of her didacticism. She is pagan
rather than positivist; a rather conventional
pagan; studying, while she wears the break-
fast cap of a British matron, the sports of
the arena. She could have taught Marcus
Aurelius much that would have opened his
eyes. One is sure, however, that her head
would have been cut off early in the week if
she had pre-existed as the story-telling princess
of the Arabian Nights. Mr. Henry James is
an experimentalist, and he dallies with the
scientific method. He has the advantage of a
manner of late so impartial that one may begin
his novels at the end and not know that one
has finished them when the commencement is
reached. With him, too, God is an abstrac-
tion. Mr. Crawford makes no philosophical
claims. He is the manager of "a pocket
theatre," yet his grasp on the eternal verities
is sure, and he philosophizes didactically on
every possible occasion; a huge book could be
made of his *dicta*. He abhors the experimental
novelist, and evidently has the old aristocratic
prejudice against science as a tool of democracy, a leveller, in fact.

To return to M. Brunetière, it is permissible
to point to him as a type — by no means an
entirely satisfactory type — of a class of men
that we badly need in English-speaking countries. There are many who explain Dante to
us, some with insight, more with unction.
There is none at present willing and capable

of interpreting the meaning of this wonderful literary and social and philosophical phenomenon, the novel, none able to appreciate its value or its strength, or to pluck out the heart of its false philosophies. It is a force, a tyranny, a terror. It may be made to serve as a key to problems that the world faces shivering.

It is not science, but it deserves scientific treatment. The province of the highest art is not to idealize, but to perfect. Science, which deals only with the exact and rational, loses its dignity when used by an author, who is an artist, to conceal the betrayal of his best.